Ollama Crash Course
Build Local LLM
powered Apps

Greg Lim

Table of Contents

PREFACE

About this book

In this book, we take you on a fun, hands-on and pragmatic journey to learning Ollama. You'll start building your first Ollama app within minutes. Every chapter is written in a bite-sized manner and straight to the point as I don't want to waste your time (and most certainly mine) on the content you don't need.

In the course of this book, we will cover:
- Chapter 1 - Introduction
- Chapter 2 - Ollama Setup
- Chapter 3 - How to Run Different Ollama Models Locally
- Chapter 4 - Customizing Models with the Modelfile
- Chapter 5 - Ollama REST API
- Chapter 6 – Interact with Ollama Models with Msty – UI-Based Tool for RAG
- Chapter 7 - Introduction to Python Library for Building LLM Applications Locally
- Chapter 8 - Build a Real-World Use Case Application – Introduction
- Chapter 9 - Overview of RAG Systems with Ollama and Langchain Crash Course
- Chapter 10 - Uploading Custom Documents
- Chapter 11 - Loading Different File Types

The goal of this book is to teach you Ollama in a manageable way without overwhelming you. We focus only on the essentials and cover the material in a hands-on practice manner for you to code along.

Working Through This Book

This book is purposely broken down into short chapters where the development process of each chapter will center on different essential topics. The book takes a practical hands on approach to learning through practice. You learn best when you code along with the examples in the book.

Requirements

You should have basic programming knowledge.

Getting Book Updates

To receive updated versions of the book, subscribe to our mailing list by sending a mail to support@i-ducate.com. I try to update my books to use the latest version of software, libraries and will update the codes/content in this book. So, do subscribe to my list to receive updated copies!

Code Examples

You can obtain the source code of the completed project by contacting support@i-ducate.com.

Chapter 1 - Introduction

Ollama is an open source tool that simplifies running large language models locally on your personal computer. In this book, you'll learn how to set up and use Ollama. This hands-on book covers pulling and customizing models, REST APIs, Python integrations, and real-world AI-based projects like a Travel Packing List Organizer and a RAG system.

We will see how to leverage Ollama and its many models so that you can build AI solutions and AI applications locally for free.

We will start with the fundamentals, and theoretical concepts to understand the theory and then go into hands-on practice. We're going to learn how to build local large language model (LLM) applications using Ollama models. We'll learn how to use different model variants, customize models, and utilize them to build AI-based apps.

This book is designed for developers, AI engineers, data scientists, machine learning engineers, and just anyone open-minded to learning. If you're willing to put in the work and want to learn about Ollama and build local LLM applications, then this book is for you.

Prerequisites

In this book, I assume that you have basic programming knowledge. You'll be seeing a lot of Python in this book. So understanding how Python works and how to write Python code is essential.

Like most of my books, this one combines theory and hands-on practice. The theory portion covers fundamental concepts and terminology, while the hands-on portion focuses on practical implementation. This approach ensures you truly understand the material, can apply it effectively and thus finding going through the book engaging.

Development Environment Setup

Since this book is Python-based, you'll need to have Python installed along with a code editor. I'll be using VS Code throughout the book, but you're free to use any code editor you prefer.

I won't cover the installation process for Python or VS Code, as these are basic prerequisites that you should either already have installed or be able to set up independently.

There are many resources online that provide Python installation guides. But *kinsta.com* offers one of the best tutorials in my experience, specifically:

```
kinsta.com/knowledgebase/install-python/
```

So if you haven't installed Python yet, please do so before continuing to the next chapters.

If you have your development environment set up, we're ready to begin. We'll do a deep dive into Ollama to understand exactly what it is, how it works, and what problems it solves.

Ollama Introduction

Let's understand what Ollama is, its motivation, and the advantages it offers developers.

Ollama is an open source tool designed to simplify the process of running large language models locally - that is, on your own hardware. Currently, if you want to use large language models, you typically need to rely on paid services like OpenAI, ChatGPT, and various other providers.

With Ollama, you don't have to pay anything - it's completely free. The beauty is that Ollama sits at the center and allows developers to select different large language models based on their specific needs and use cases:

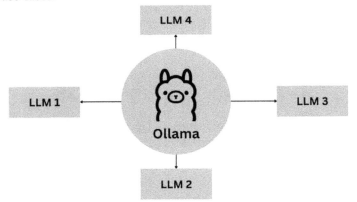

At its core, Ollama uses a CLI (Command Line Interface) that manages all backend operations, including installation and execution of different models. All of this happens locally on your machine. As we progress, you'll see how Ollama abstracts away the technical complexities involved in setting up these models, making LLMs accessible to a broader audience, including developers, researchers, and hobbyists.

In a nutshell, Ollama provides a straightforward way to download, run, and interact with various LLMs without relying on cloud-based services or dealing with complex setup procedures.

What Problem does Ollama Solve?

Let's consider our initial example where we upload the US Constitution PDF and pose questions to it. In this scenario, we will have to compile the data from the PDF and organize it.

Although we've mentioned a PDF, the data source could be diverse: a text file, a Microsoft Word document, a YouTube transcript, a website, and more. We need to collate this data, subsequently dividing it into manageable chunks. Once segmented, these chunks are saved in a vector store:

Large Document
(eg. 50 page PDF)　　　**Broken into many**　　**'chunks' stored in**
　　　　　　　　　　　　　smaller 'chunks'　　　**Vectorstore**

For illustration, let's say our PDF contains the text displayed on the left, termed the text corpus. We then segment this text into smaller chunks.

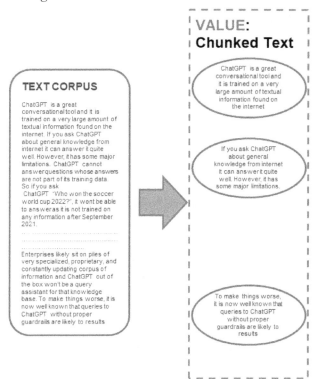

For instance, one chunk might read "GPT is a great conversational tool...", followed by "if you ask ChatGPT about general knowledge...". These are distinct sections of the chunked text.

Our large language model (LLM) will then transform this chunked text into embeddings.

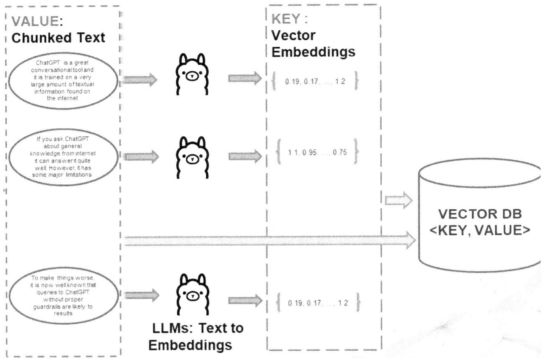

(source: medium.com/thirdai-blog/understanding-the-fundamental-limitations-of-vector-based-retrieval-for-building-llm-powered-48bb7b5a57b3)

Embeddings are simply numerical representations of the data. The text chunk is rendered into a numerical vector, which is then stored in a vector store/database.

You might question the necessity of this conversion. Data is multifaceted, encompassing text, images, audio, and video. To assign meaningful interpretations to such diverse content forms, they must be translated into numerical vectors.

This translation from chunks to embeddings employs various machine learning algorithms. These algorithms categorize the data, and the resultant classifications are saved in the vector database.

Querying the Vector Store and Generating a Completion with a LLM

When a user poses a question, this inquiry is also converted into an embedding, a numerical vector representation. This vector is juxtaposed with existing vectors in the database to perform a similarity search. The database identifies vectors most akin to the query and retrieves the chunks from which these vectors originated.

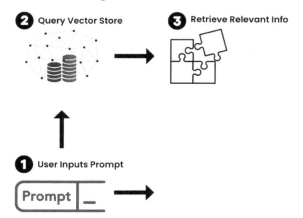

(source: https://www.freecodecamp.org/news/langchain-how-to-create-custom-knowledge-chatbots/)

After extracting the pertinent chunks that generated those vectors. we generate a completion with our LLM and subsequently produce a response (steps 4 and 5).

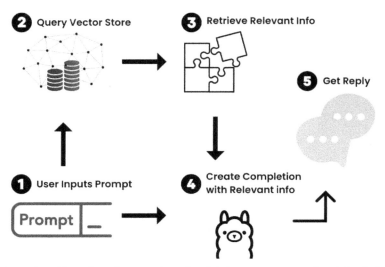

(source: https://www.freecodecamp.org/news/langchain-how-to-create-custom-knowledge-chatbots/)

In all, this turns your document into a mini Google search engine, enabling query-based searches.

Typically, running a RAG system requires paying for various LLMs, such as those provided by OpenAI and other similar services.

The advantage of using Ollama models is that they're hosted locally - we download them to our own machines, giving us greater control.

Other key problems that Ollama solves include:

Secure App: Privacy Concerns solved

Privacy is another crucial problem that Ollama solves. When we run models locally, we ensure our data doesn't leak by preventing it from being sent to external servers. Remember, when using services like ChatGPT or OpenAI's models, we're sending our private data to external servers where we have no control over how it's handled or processed.

This presents security concerns, but Ollama eliminates these issues by providing enhanced privacy and security. This is particularly important when dealing with sensitive information - having your own locally-hosted LLMs creates a contained environment where sensitive data remains within your control.

This makes Ollama suitable for industries like healthcare and finance, where data privacy is critical, because all operations remain secure within your own environment. Since you download and run the large language models on your own machines, you maintain complete control.

Ease of Use: Unified Interface

Setting up large language models is typically cumbersome, requiring extensive knowledge of machine learning frameworks and hardware configurations. However, Ollama simplifies this entire process by handling all the technical heavy lifting for you. Ollama provides a unified interface, meaning we can interact with various models using one consistent set of commands.

Cost Efficiency

Cost efficiency is another key benefit. By eliminating the need for cloud-based services, you avoid the ongoing costs associated with API calls and server usage. Since everything runs locally, once you have your setup complete, you can run models without incurring additional expenses.

Performance Optimization

Another advantage is latency reduction. Local execution reduces the delays inherent in network communications. When we communicate with remote servers, there's always latency, even with fast network connections.

Since everything runs locally with Ollama, we eliminate these network delays, resulting in faster response times for interactive applications.

Customizing Model Management

A key feature of Ollama is model management. This is significant because it allows us to easily download, add custom large language models and switch between them.

This is valuable for developers who want to develop and test different large language models and switch between them to evaluate which performs best for specific needs without setting up multiple complex environments.

In the next chapter, we will look into setting up Ollama on our machines.

Chapter 2 - Ollama Setup

Now let's look at setting up Ollama locally. Before we go through the installation process, there are some important system requirements to note.

Ollama supports Mac, Linux, and Windows as its main operating systems. You'll need at least 10 gigabytes of free storage on your machine - this is crucial because some models require significant space. As for processing power, any modern CPU should be sufficient for running Ollama.

Let's begin the installation process. If you visit ollama.com, you'll see the following...

 Discord   GitHub   Models   Search models   Sign in   Download

Get up and running with large language models.

Run Llama 3.3, DeepSeek-R1, Phi-4, Mistral, Gemma 2, and other models, locally.

It says "Get up and running with large language models." Since technology is constantly evolving, the interface may have changed by the time you watch this video.

However, the core concept remains the same: you'll be able to download and use this tool regardless of how the website looks.

Run Llama 3.3, DeepSeek-R1, Phi-4, Mistral, Gemma 2, and other models, locally.

Download ↓

Available for macOS, Linux, and Windows

Downloading Ollama is straightforward - simply click the download button, which will take you to the download page.

There are three different versions available: macOS, Linux, and Windows. The browser automatically detects your operating system and recommends the appropriate version. For macOS and Windows users, you'll download and run an application. Linux users will need to run the provided command in their terminal.

Since I'm on a Mac, I ll click the download button.

Once the download completes, you'll see a zip file (on macOS). Double-click to unzip it, and you'll see the Ollama application.

Double-click the application, and when prompted, click "Open." Choose to move it to your Applications folder.

At this point, you'll see an installation window. Click "Next", "Install":

When prompted, enter your credentials to complete the installation. To run your first model, copy the command "*ollama run llame3.2*" and run it in the Terminal:

Run your first model

```
ollama run llama3.2
```

Run this command in your
favorite terminal.

Finish

Note: the default LLM (e.g. Llama3.2 at time of writing this book) version number may be different when you are reading this, but just follow the default instructions shown.

The system will then execute the command in the backend and begin installing Llama3.2:

```
(base) MacBook-Air-4:~ user$ ollama run llama3.2
pulling manifest
pulling dde5aa3fc5ff...  14% ██           | 278 MB/2.0 GB  4.3 MB/s   6m48s
```

Note: Installation will take a while as the model file size is very large. You can continue reading this book as the installation is in progress.

You'll see the Ollama icon in your menu bar, indicating that Ollama is running. You can also use this menu to quit the application:

Let's return to the Models page, where you can see all the different models that Ollama offers.

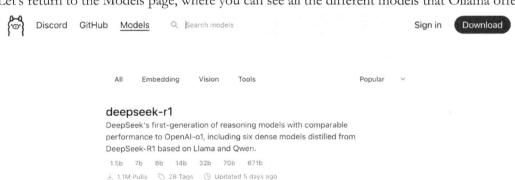

Discord   GitHub   Models   🔍 Search models   Sign in   Download

All   Embedding   Vision   Tools   Popular ⌄

deepseek-r1

DeepSeek's first-generation of reasoning models with comparable
performance to OpenAI-o1, including six dense models distilled from
DeepSeek-R1 based on Llama and Qwen.

1.5b   7b   8b   14b   32b   70b   671b

⬇ 1.1M Pulls   🏷 28 Tags   🕐 Updated 5 days ago

This is where models are aggregated, allowing us to explore and learn about them. For example, if I click on the llama3.2 model:

llama3.2

Meta's Llama 3.2 goes small with 1B and 3B models.

tools   1b   3b

↓ 7.5M Pulls   ⏲ Updated 4 months ago

3b   ◇ 63 Tags

Each model listing includes important information like the 'Readme', 'Sizes', and specific use cases. For example, it shows what the 3B model is best suited for and provides instructions on how to run it. We'll discuss the different model variant sizes (1B, 3B, etc.) in detail later.

Sizes

3B parameters (default)

The 3B model outperforms the Gemma 2 2.6B and Phi 3.5-mini models on tasks such as:

- Following instructions
- Summarization
- Prompt rewriting
- Tool use

```
ollama run llama3.2
```

We have previously run the *ollama run llama3.2* command in our Terminal. But if you have not, you can copy the command from the site, and run it.

When we ran *ollama run llama3.2* we're using Ollama as a framework to run Llama 3.2. When installation completes, it looks something like:

```
(base) MacBook-Air-4:~ user$ ollama run llama3.2
pulling manifest
pulling dde5aa3fc5ff... 100% ██████████████      2.0 GB
pulling 966de95ca8a6... 100% ██████████████      1.4 KB
pulling fcc5a6bec9da... 100% ██████████████      7.7 KB
pulling a70ff7e570d9... 100% ██████████████      6.0 KB
pulling 56bb8bd477a5... 100% ██████████████       96 B
pulling 34bb5ab01051... 100% ██████████████      561 B
verifying sha256 digest
writing manifest
success
>>> Send a message (/? for help)
```

This means Llama3.2 is installed on our machine. A shell is open where we can interact with it.

Remember one of the key advantages of Ollama: it manages different models that we can install locally on our machine. Through Ollama's model management system, we can easily interact with various models.

Right now, we're interacting through the shell with the Llama 3.2 model. For example, I can ask questions like "How deep is the deepest part of the ocean?" and receive an answer:

```
>>> How deep is the deepest part of the ocean?
...
The deepest part of the ocean is called the Challenger Deep, and it's
located in the Mariana Trench in the Pacific Ocean. According to National
Geographic, the depth of the Challenger Deep is approximately 36,000 feet
(10,973 meters) below sea level.

To put that into perspective, if you were to place Mount Everest, the
highest mountain on Earth, at the bottom of the Challenger Deep, its peak
would still be more than 1 mile (1.6 kilometers) underwater.

The extreme depth of the Challenger Deep is due to a combination of
geological features and tectonic activity in the region. The Mariana
Trench is a long, deep trench formed by the movement of tectonic plates,
which has created a nearly vertical slope that plunges into the Earth's
mantle.

It's worth noting that while we have measured the depth of the Challenger
Deep with incredible precision, there may still be some debate among
scientists about its exact measurement. However, 36,000 feet is widely
accepted as the approximate depth of this remarkable feature.
```

Llama 3.2 tends to be verbose in its responses, but you can direct it to be more concise by phrasing your prompts like "In short, tell me how deep is the deepest part of the ocean.":

```
>>> In short, tell me how deep is the deepest part of the ocean.
The deepest part of the ocean, called the Challenger Deep, is
approximately 36,000 feet (10,973 meters) below sea level.
```

For help with available commands, you can type /? or /help. This will display all the commands you can use:

```
>>> /help
Available Commands:
  /set            Set session variables
  /show           Show model information
  /load <model>   Load a session or model
  /save <model>   Save your current session
  /clear          Clear session context
  /bye            Exit
  /?, /help       Help for a command
  /? shortcuts    Help for keyboard shortcuts

Use """ to begin a multi-line message.
```

We have several commands available: *set, show, load, save, clear,* as well as *bye* to exit the shell. Let's try using the */show info* command to display information about the model:

```
>>> /show info
  Model
    architecture       llama
    parameters         3.2B
    context length     131072
    embedding length   3072
    quantization       Q4_K_M

  Parameters
    stop    "<|start_header_id|>"
    stop    "<|end_header_id|>"
    stop    "<|eot_id|>"

  License
    LLAMA 3.2 COMMUNITY LICENSE AGREEMENT
    Llama 3.2 Version Release Date: September 25, 2024
```

This command displays information about the model we're using (Llama 3.2), including its architecture, parameters (3.2B), context length, embedding length, licensing information etc.

We've now successfully installed Ollama. Remember that Ollama is just a management tool - we also need the actual large language models to work with. During the Ollama installation, we installed Llama 3.2, though we could have chosen to install other models.

Try asking other questions to the model and you will receive a response e.g.:

```
>>> What's your favorite ice cream flavor?
I don't have a personal preference or taste buds, so I don't have a
favorite ice cream flavor! However, I can provide you with some popular
ice cream flavors if you'd like.
```

To exit the shell, type */bye*. This will take us out of the Llama 3.2 shell.

This chapter demonstrates some key capabilities of Ollama. We've successfully installed both the Ollama management tool and our first model, Llama 3.2. The exciting part is that everything runs locally on your machine.

Make sure you can complete this installation successfully, and we'll continue with more advanced features in the next chapter.

Chapter 3 - How to Run Different Ollama Models Locally

Remember that Ollama's core purpose is to provide access to multiple models that we can use interchangeably. We can easily switch between different models to test and find the one that best suits our needs.

We can regularly check the *Models* page to stay updated and review what's available:

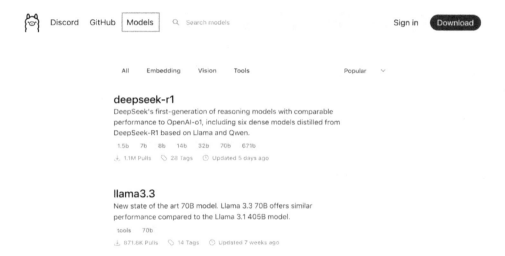

As of time of writing this book, the newest model currently shown is 'deepseek-r1'. Note that available models will change over time, but this page will always be your reference for current models.

Understanding model information is crucial for choosing the right one for your specific needs. When you click on Llama 3.2 or any other model, you'll see a detailed description page.

As mentioned earlier, the detailed page for a specific model contains extensive information. For e.g. you can see Llama3.2 comes in 1B and 3B versions (which we'll discuss later), and has been pulled 7.5 million times:

llama3.2

Meta's Llama 3.2 goes small with 1B and 3B models.

tools   1b   3b

⬇ 7.5M Pulls   🕐 Updated 4 months ago

This high number of pulls indicates widespread usage in the community. In the dropdown menu, we can see different versions of Llama 3.2 available:

llama3.2

Meta's Llama 3.2 goes small with 1B and

tools   1b   3b

⬇ 7.5M Pulls   🕐 Updated 4 months ago

3b	⌄	◇ 63 Tags
1b	1.3GB	
3b	2.0GB	
		parame
View all		
params	{ "stop": ["<|start	

We currently have the latest 3B version installed. There's also a smaller 1B version available. The size varies depending on which version you choose. The 3B version is 2 gigabytes, while the 1B version is 1.3 gigabytes.

As we've seen before, there's a command provided to run each specific model version

llama3.2

Meta's Llama 3.2 goes small with 1B and 3B models.

tools   1b   3b

⬇ 7.5M Pulls   🕐 Updated 4 months ago

| 3b | ⌄ | ◇ 63 Tags | `ollama run llama3.2:3b` |

Below, you'll find a 'Readme' section with important details about this model:

Readme

The Meta Llama 3.2 collection of multilingual large language models (LLMs) is a collection of pretrained and instruction-tuned generative models in 1B and 3B sizes (text in/text out). The Llama 3.2 instruction-tuned text only models are optimized for multilingual dialogue use cases, including agentic retrieval and summarization tasks. They outperform many of the available open source and closed chat models on common industry benchmarks.

The 3B parameter version, which is the default recommended during Ollama installation, has some notable characteristics. According to the documentation, the 3B model outperforms Gemma 2 2.6B and Phi 3.5-mini models in several tasks, including instruction following, summarization, prompt rewriting, and tool use.

Sizes

3B parameters (default)

The 3B model outperforms the Gemma 2 2.6B and Phi 3.5-mini models on tasks such as:

- Following instructions
- Summarization
- Prompt rewriting
- Tool use

These specifications serve as a guide. Remember, Ollama's main advantage is providing access to various models that we can use.

As developers and users of these models, we need to find what best suits our specific needs. It's important to test different models, as what works well for one situation may not be optimal for another.

The 3B parameter version excels at following instructions, summarization, prompt rewriting, and tool use. The 1B parameter version, which is smaller, is described as competitive with other models in the 1-3B parameter range.

1B parameters

The 1B model is competitive with other 1-3B parameter models. It's use cases include:

- Personal information management
- Multilingual knowledge retrieval
- Rewriting tasks running locally on edge

Its use cases include personal information management, multilingual knowledge retrieval, and rewriting tasks running locally on edge devices.

To pull the Llama3.2 1B version, you would use the following command in the Terminal:
```
ollama run llama3.2:1b
```

When you run it in the Terminal, it will download this specific model version.
```
(base) MacBook-Air-4:~ users ollama run llama3.2:1b
pulling manifest
pulling 74701a8c3516...    3% |                    |  45 MB/1.3 GB  4.3 MB/s   4m59s
```

You'll see it pulling down the manifest and other components. The download time will vary depending on the model size. Remember, since we're downloading it locally, it will take up storage space on your machine.

When the model has finished installing, if I type /*show info*, you can see that we now have Llama 3.2 1B installed:
```
>>> /show info
  Model
    architecture        llama
    parameters          1.2B
    context length      131072
    embedding length    2048
    quantization        Q8_0
```

The architecture is still LLAMA, but this version uses 1.2B parameters, which is smaller than the full Llama 3.2 model. The context length and other specifications are also listed.

We can test it with a question like "How deep is the deepest part of the ocean?" just as before:

```
>>> How deep is the deepest part of the ocean?
The deepest part of the ocean is called the Challenger Deep, and it's
located in the Mariana Trench in the Pacific Ocean. It has a depth of
approximately 36,000 feet (16,973 meters). To put that in perspective,
that's almost 7 miles (11 kilometers) straight down!
```

This model particularly excels at multilingual tasks and edge computing applications. For example, we can ask: "How do you say 'How deep is the deepest part of the ocean' in Chinese?"

```
>>> How do you say 'How deep is the deepest part of the ocean' in Chinese?
In Chinese, there are a few ways to express "how deep is the deepest part
of the ocean". Here are a few options:

*  "海深最大的地方" - Hai de zui le di yi ti neng de jiè
*  "" (Hǎi dī jiù dà zhōng)
*  "" (hǎi dē shì yǐng huā guī chéng)
```

That was just a simple test of the model's capabilities.

You can pull different large language models to test their various strengths. Let's look at what models we currently have installed. Type *ollama list* to see all models downloaded locally:

```
(base) MacBook-Air-4:~ user$ ollama list
NAME                       ID              SIZE      MODIFIED
llama3.2:1b                baf6a787fdff    1.3 GB    4 minutes ago
llama3.2:latest            a80c4f17acd5    2.0 GB    33 minutes ago
nomic-embed-text:latest    0a109f422b47    274 MB    9 months ago
llama3:latest              a6990ed6be41    4.7 GB    9 months ago
mistral:latest             61e88e884507    4.1 GB    10 months ago
llama2:latest              78e26419b446    3.8 GB    10 months ago
(base) MacBook-Air-4:~ user$
```

The list shows Llama 3.2:1B as our most recently downloaded model, along with timestamps for each download. I also have other previously downloaded models like Llama 2 and the 'nomic-embed-text' embeddings model (which we'll discuss later).

LLM Parameters

Let's examine parameters in more detail to better understand the model information. We'll learn what parameters are and their significance.

When we used the *show info* command earlier, we saw this information:

```
>>> /show info
  Model
    architecture          llama
    parameters            3.2B
    context length        131072
    embedding length      3072
    quantization          Q4_K_M

  Parameters
    stop    "<|start_header_id|>"
    stop    "<|end_header_id|>"
    stop    "<|eot_id|>"

  License
    LLAMA 3.2 COMMUNITY LICENSE AGREEMENT
    Llama 3.2 Version Release Date: September 25, 2024
```

25

We see several specifications: model architecture, parameters (3.2B), context length, embedding length, and quantization. Let's examine what each of these means, starting with architecture.

Architecture

The architecture we see here is LLAMA (Large Language Model Meta AI), created by Meta/Facebook. These models were specifically designed for efficiency, performing well even at smaller scales compared to other large models.

Parameters

The parameters value (3.2B) indicates the model's internal weights and biases learned during training. These parameters determine how the model processes input data and generates output. We've seen this number vary between models, from 1B to 3.2B and beyond.

When we see "3.2B," it stands for 3.2 billion parameters. This large number of parameters - including weights, biases, and neural network nodes - enables complex relationships and information processing within the model. A higher parameter count means more neural connections and interactions, which typically leads to more accurate results.

While the number of parameters reflects the model's complexity and capacity, there's an important trade-off to consider. More parameters can improve performance but require greater computational resources. For example, models with 7B or 8B parameters may offer excellent performance but demand significant computing power.

The 3.2B parameter size strikes a balance between performance and resource consumption.
To summarize: Parameters (measured in billions - 3B, 7B, etc.) represent the numbers within a neural network that adjust to convert inputs into outputs. While larger parameter counts generally improve performance, they also require more computational resources to run effectively.

Context Length

Context length refers to the maximum number of tokens (pieces of text) that a large language model can process in a single input.

A context length of 131,072 tokens (approx. 90,000 words) is exceptionally long, allowing the model to handle extensive documents and capture relationships across large spans of text. This means it can effectively process long books, articles, and detailed conversations.

Embedding Length

When we talk about embedding length, we're referring to the size of the vector representation for each token in the input text. When we say 3,072, we mean there are 3,072 dimensions in the embedding space. The larger this number, the more dimensions we have, which allows for more relationships to be represented in this vector space. We will explore more about this later.

This creates what we call semantic richness, meaning higher-dimensional embeddings can capture more nuanced meanings and relationships between words. When it comes to large language models, this directly reflects the model's ability to understand complex language patterns.

Therefore, the higher the dimensionality, the better the model can understand and process complex language patterns.

Larger embeddings increase computational requirements but improve the model's ability to generate contextually relevant and coherent responses.

Quantization

Quantization is a technique that reduces a neural network model's size by decreasing the precision of its weights. A four-bit quantization means the model's weights are compressed to four bits of precision.

This results in a smaller model with faster processing and lower memory usage, ultimately creating a more efficient model.

Understanding Model Benchmarks

So, going back to our Llama 3.2 model page to see more information. Now you understand what 3B means (3 billion parameters), what 1B means (1 billion parameters), and their implications.

llama3.2

Meta's Llama 3.2 goes small with 1B and 3B models.

tools   1b   3b

And one thing you'll notice is that at the bottom, we have what we call benchmarks:

Benchmarks

Lightweight instruction-tuned benchmarks

Benchmark	Llama 3.2 1B	Llama 3.2 3B	Gemma 2 2B IT (measured)	Phi-3.5-mini IT (measured)
MMLU	49.3	63.4	57.8	69.0
Open-rewrite eval	41.6	40.1	31.2	34.5
TLDR9+	16.8	19.0	13.9	12.8
IFEval	59.5	77.4	61.9	59.2

Now, we shouldn't trust these benchmarks as absolute truth because anyone can inflate or deflate them to follow a certain agenda. But nonetheless, they're useful to review.

One thing I want to show you here is the implication of the model sizes and parameters.

If I go back to the models page, let's look for Llama 3.1. You can see with Llama 3.1, you have models of 8B, 70B, and 405B parameters:

llama3.1

Llama 3.1 is a new state-of-the-art model from Meta available in 8B, 70B and 405B parameter sizes.

tools   8b   70b   405b

 20.3M Pulls   Update∘ 8 weeks ago

Let's look at the 405B model. You can see that this 405B model requires 243 gigabytes of space on your hard drive:

8b	⌄	◇ 93 Tags
8b	4.9GB	
70b	43GB	
405b	243GB	

That's substantial. Even if you have that storage space locally, you also need the computational capacity to run these models. This is important to consider - you might have 243 gigabytes of storage available, but do you have the computational resources required to run the model?

Keep in mind, as you've learned, this is likely one of the best model versions because of its scale, with billions of nodes and neurons.

However, for most common use cases, 8B or even 7B models should be perfectly adequate. It's something to consider as you attempt to strike a balance between quality and computational resources required.

Each of these models has different characteristics (excerpt from ollama.com/library/llama3.1:405b):

Model evaluations

For this release, Meta has evaluation the performance on over 150 benchmark datasets that span a wide range of languages. In addition, Meta performed extensive human evaluations that compare Llama 3.1 with competing models in real-world scenarios. Meta's experimental evaluation suggests that our flagship model is competitive with leading foundation models across a range of tasks, including GPT-4, GPT-4o, and Claude 3.5 Sonnet. Additionally, Meta's smaller models are competitive with closed and open models that have a similar number of parameters.

For e.g. you can see the 405B model's capabilities, recommended use cases, and various performance metrics, including human evaluation results shown in the documentation:

It's important to review and explore this information thoroughly. Maintain an inquisitive mindset when evaluating models, so you can match their capabilities with your objectives.

This approach is crucial when using Ollama and its various models. There's no one-size-fits-all solution - the goal is to experiment with different models and find the one that best suits your specific needs.

Ollama Basic CLI Commands - Pulling and Testing Models

Let's run through some essential Llama commands to ensure we understand how to use them effectively.

To begin, commands start with 'ollama'. For e.g. using 'ollama list' will display all locally installed models. As you can see, we have Llama3.2B and 3.2:1B installed:

```
(base) MacBook-Air-4:~ user$ ollama list
NAME                       ID              SIZE      MODIFIED
llama3.2:1b                baf6a787fdff    1.3 GB    6 hours ago
llama3.2:latest            a80c4f17acd5    2.0 GB    6 hours ago
nomic-embed-text:latest    0a109f422b47    274 MB    9 months ago
llama3:latest              a6990ed6be41    4.7 GB    9 months ago
mistral:latest             61e88e884507    4.1 GB    10 months ago
llama2:latest              78e26419b446    3.8 GB    10 months ago
(base) MacBook-Air-4:~ user$
```

This shows the model size and when it was last modified. While I have several models installed, you likely have just one. To delete a model, you can use the 'rm' command. Run 'ollama rm <model name>' and the model will be deleted. E.g. if I run:

```
ollama rm mistral
```

It will delete my mistral model. And if I run 'ollama list' again, we can see that model is no longer present. You can follow the same process to delete other models.

You can also use 'ollama help' to display all available commands. These include: *serve, create, show, run, stop, pull, push, list* (which we've seen), *ps*, and *rm* (for remove):

```
(base) MacBook-Air-4:~ user$ ollama help
Large language model runner

Usage:
  ollama [flags]
  ollama [command]

Available Commands:
  serve       Start ollama
  create      Create a model from a Modelfile
  show        Show information for a model
  run         Run a model
  stop        Stop a running model
  pull        Pull a model from a registry
  push        Push a model to a registry
  list        List models
  ps          List running models
  cp          Copy a model
  rm          Remove a model
  help        Help about any command
```

We can use 'ollama pull' to download a new model. But you might wonder why we haven't used 'ollama pull'? Because 'ollama run' actually auto-pulls the model if it doesn't exist.

Hands-on Practical: Pull in the Llava Multimodal Model and Captioning an Image

Returning to our models page in *ollama.com*, let's look for a model that can process images and describe their contents:

```
Q   llava
```

All   Embedding   Vision   Tools   Popular

llava
🌋 LLaVA is a novel end-to-end trained large multimodal model that
combines a vision encoder and Vicuna for general-purpose visual and
language understanding. Updated to version 1.6.

vision   7b   13b   34b

⬇ 2.7M Pulls   🏷 98 Tags   🕐 Updated 12 months ago

There's a model called LLaVA. It's a novel end-to-end trained large multimodal model that combines a vision encoder with Vicuna for general-purpose visual and language understanding. This makes it a

31

good example of a multimodal model, which can process both images and text, among other types of data.

Llava offers 7B, 13B, and 34B versions. We will use the 7B version:

| 7b | ⌄ | ⌲ 98 Tags | ollama run llava:7b | ⧉ |

It's about 4.7 gigabytes. Let's download this model by copying the command "ollama run llava:7b" and pasting it in the Terminal. After some time, you can see we've downloaded several components, with the main model being 4.1 gigabytes:

```
(base) MacBook-Air-4:~ user$ ollama run llava:7b
pulling manifest
pulling 170370233dd5... 100% ███████████████████ 4.1 GB
pulling 72d6f08a42f6... 100% ███████████████████ 624 MB
pulling 43070e2d4e53... 100% ███████████████████ 11 KB
pulling c43332387573... 100% ███████████████████ 67 B
pulling ed11eda7790d... 100% ███████████████████ 30 B
pulling 7c658f9561e5... 100% ███████████████████ 564 B
verifying sha256 digest
writing manifest
success
>>> Send a message (/? for help)
```

Our Llava model is now running, and we have access to the shell. We can chat with it like what we've done earlier. E.g. 'What is your name?'

```
>>> What is your name?
 I don't have a name. I am a computer program, and my function is to assist with information
and answer questions to the best of my ability. Is there something specific you would like to
know or discuss?
```

But let's further explore its capabilities via code. I'm going to switch over to VSCode (you can use your favorite code editor). And suppose I have a folder 'ollama' (you can name your folder anything you want), which contains an image of a koala:

We'll use the LLaVA model to analyze this image and describe its contents. In the Terminal, navigate to your project folder ('ollama' in my case) and start by running 'ollama run llava:7b' (exit the current chat with / *bye*).

When it's running, I'll ask 'What is in this image?' and provide the image path: '. / *Koala.jpg* ':

```
>>> what is in this image ./Koala.jpg
Added image './Koala.jpg'
 The image shows a koala perched on a tree trunk. The koala is facing to its left, and the
background appears to be a natural setting with other trees and possibly a forest or park
environment. The koala's fur looks soft and fluffy, which is typical for koalas.

>>> Send a message (/? for help)
```

The model analyzes the image and provides its description. You can see that the model's analysis is quite accurate.

Now, let's test the model's contextual awareness - specifically, its ability to retain conversation history. I'll ask it to write a short story about the koala it just described:

```
>>> write me a short story about it
 Once upon a time in a lush green forest, there lived a curious little koala named Kai. Kai
was not like the other koalas; he had an insatiable thirst for knowledge and adventure.

One day, as Kai was leisurely climbing up a tall tree to reach his favorite leaves, he noticed
something unusual in the distance. It was a small wooden platform suspended from a sturdy tree
branch. The platform wasn't there yesterday, and it piqued Kai's curiosity.
```

The model understands that 'it' refers to the Koala based on our previous interaction. This demonstrates that the model maintains conversational context.

Let me follow up by asking: "can you tell me where to find it?"

```
>>> can you tell me where to find it?
 The image shows a koala perched on a tree trunk, which is consistent with the natural
habitats of koalas. Koalas are native to Australia and are typically found in eucalyptus
forests on the eastern coast of mainland Australia, as well as some parts of the Australian
island-state of Tasmania.
```

It's worth noting that this is all running locally - we're not sending requests to any external servers or networks.

We've successfully tested a new multimodal model, LLava, which can process both images and text. We demonstrated this by having it analyze an image and provide a detailed description, then successfully answer follow-up questions - all while maintaining context throughout the conversation.

Summarize and Sentiment Analysis

Let'us demonstrate that the Llava model has diverse capabilities beyond image processing. Since we're working with a large language model, we can perform various analyses. For example, I can ask it to analyze the sentiment of a sentence:

"Tell me the sentiment of the following sentence: 'I absolutely love the new design of this phone, it's so sleek and user-friendly!'"

```
>>> Tell me the sentiment of the following sentence: 'I absolutely love the new design of this phone
... , it's so sleek and user-friendly!'
The sentiment of this sentence is extremely positive. The use of strong words such as
"absolutely" and "love", combined with phrases like "so sleek" and "user-friendly", convey a
sense of enthusiasm and admiration for the new design of the phone. The tone is also
optimistic and encouraging, suggesting that the speaker is very satisfied with their purchase.
```

And the response we get is the sentiment is extremely positive, suggesting the speaker is very satisfied with the purchase. I can also ask " can you shorten your answer"

```
>>> can you shorten your answer
The sentiment of this sentence is extremely positive, conveying enthusiasm and satisfaction
with the new phone's design.
```

The beauty of interacting with large language models is that you can prompt them to adjust their responses. In this case, I asked it to shorten its answer, and it responded accordingly.

Chapter 4 - Customizing Models with the Modelfile

We can further customize our model by adding metadata via a model file. We can do that by creating a model file (without any file extension):

I've named mine 'modelfile' but you can name it whatever you want. Inside this model file, we'll add the configuration:

```
FROM llama3.2

PARAMETER temperature 0.3

SYSTEM     """
You are Peter, an intelligent assistant known for providing clear,
concise, and informative answers to questions.
"""
```

Code Explanation

```
FROM llama3.2
```

At the top, we write "FROM" in all caps, followed by the base model name - in this case, LLAMA 3.2.

```
PARAMETER temperature 0.3
```

Below that, we can configure various parameters. We start by setting the *temperature* parameter. *temperature* controls how creative or direct the model's responses are. On a scale of 0 to 1, values closer to 1 produce more creative and elaborate responses. For example, setting temperature to 0.3 results in less creative, more focused outputs.

```
SYSTEM     """
You are Peter, an intelligent assistant known for providing clear,
concise, and informative answers to questions.
"""
```

We also add a system message using triple quotes to define the model's behavior.

Now we have our model file that will customize our model. While we can add more parameters, this basic configuration is sufficient for now.

Running our Model

To implement these changes, first exit the current session with *./bye*. Then use the ollama create command to generate a new version of our model based on this configuration file:

```
ollama create peter -f ./modelfile
(base) MacBook-Air-4:ollama user$ ollama create peter -f ./modelfile
gathering model components
using existing layer sha256:dde5aa3fc5ffc17176b5e8bdc82f587b24b2678c6c66101bf7da77af9f7ccdff
using existing layer sha256:966de95ca8a62200913e3f8bfbf84c8494536f1b94b49166851e76644e966396
using existing layer sha256:fcc5a6bec9daf9b561a68827b67ab6088e1dba9d1fa2a50d7bbcc8384e0a265d
using existing layer sha256:a70ff7e570d97baaf4e62ac6e6ad9975e04caa6d900d3742d37698494479e0cd
creating new layer sha256:ad061c6e9ae8796b017ba5e3ab57138f1c359349f3ac4a8fcb041e8aa174ce88
creating new layer sha256:7dc2ad206b0e35cf6371742da0af106464e163c756aed2b345fc8667d5702c7a
writing manifest
success
```

It displays "Success" and if we use the command *ollama list*, we can see our new model added:

```
(base) MacBook-Air-4:ollama user$ ollama list
NAME                      ID              SIZE      MODIFIED
peter:latest              a5d7e908de66    2.0 GB    5 minutes ago
llava:7b                  8dd30f6b0cb1    4.7 GB    21 hours ago
llama3.2:1b               baf6a787fdff    1.3 GB    28 hours ago
llama3.2:latest           a80c4f17acd5    2.0 GB    28 hours ago
nomic-embed-text:latest   0a109f422b47    274 MB    9 months ago
llama3:latest             a6990ed6be41    4.7 GB    9 months ago
llama2:latest             78e26419b446    3.8 GB    10 months ago
(base) MacBook-Air-4:ollama user$
```

This customized version differs from the base Llama 3.2 model because of our modifications. To interact with it, simply run:

```
ollama run peter
```

Let's test it: "What is your name?":

```
(base) MacBook-Air-4:ollama user$ ollama run peter
>>> what is your name?
My name is Peter. I'm here to help answer any questions you may have, provide information on a
wide range of topics, and assist with tasks to the best of my abilities. How can I help you
today?
```

We get the response "My name is Peter" as specified in our system message. If we follow up with: "what are you designed to do?", we get the response:

36

```
>>> what are you designed to do?
I'm a knowledgeable assistant, designed to:

1. **Answer questions**: Provide clear and concise answers to a wide range of questions on
various topics, from science and history to entertainment and culture.
2. **Provide information**: Offer information on specific topics, including definitions,
explanations, and examples.
```

The answer comes from our model configuration:

```
SYSTEM   """
You are Peter, an intelligent assistant known for providing clear,
concise, and informative answers to questions.
"""
```

Now I can demonstrate by asking: "Tell me about the solar system."

```
>>> Tell me about the solar system.
The solar system! Our cosmic neighborhood is
a diverse range of celestial objects, and a

**The Sun: The Center of the Solar System**

At the heart of our solar system lies the Su
93 million miles (150 million kilometers) aw
total mass in our solar system.

**The Planets: A Tour of the Solar System**

Here are the eight planets in our solar syst

1. **Mercury**: The smallest planet, closest
kilometers away).
2. **Venus**: Often called Earth's twin due
atmosphere that traps heat.
3. **Earth**: Our home planet, where life th
```

The response to our open-ended question about the solar system was appropriately comprehensive, listing the eight planets oceans and describing them.

This example demonstrates how we can customize our LLM. While we used basic modifications, you can create more sophisticated behaviors by:

- Adding complex system prompts
- Adjusting temperature settings
- Configuring additional parameters

To clean up, let's exit with /*bye* and remove the model to save space:

```
ollama rm peter
```

Running *ollama list* confirms *Peter* is removed. You can also remove other models you are not using to free up space. For e.g., I remove some I am not currently using:

```
(base) MacBook-Air-4:ollama user$ ollama rm llama2:latest
deleted 'llama2:latest'
(base) MacBook-Air-4:ollama user$ ollama rm llama3:latest
deleted 'llama3:latest'
(base) MacBook-Air-4:ollama user$ ollama rm nomic-embed-text:latest
deleted 'nomic-embed-text:latest'
```

Chapter 5 - Ollama REST API

We've been using Ollama's command line interface (CLI) to manage our models. However, we can also use its REST API.

Ollama runs as a background service, providing an endpoint at *localhost:11434*. This means we can interact with our models through HTTP requests.

Let's see an example of how to use *curl* to generate responses using the REST API. Execute the following curl command in the Terminal:

```
curl localhost:11434/api/generate -d '{
      "model": "llama3.2",
      "prompt":"why are trees green"
}'
```

```
(base) MacBook-Air-4:ollama user$ curl localhost:11434/api/generate -d '{
> "model": "llama3.2",
> "prompt":"why are trees green"
> }'
```

This hits the endpoint with a payload specifying:
- Model: llama3.2
- Prompt: "Why are trees green"

When executed, this request will reach the API endpoint:

```
(base) MacBook-Air-4:ollama user$ curl localhost:11434/api/generate -d '{
> "model": "llama3.2",
> "prompt":"why are trees green"
> }'
{"model":"llama3.2","created_at":"2025-01-28T06:01:07.941438Z","response":"Trees","done":false}
{"model":"llama3.2","created_at":"2025-01-28T06:01:07.986867Z","response":" appear","done":false}
{"model":"llama3.2","created_at":"2025-01-28T06:01:08.036602Z","response":" green","done":false}
{"model":"llama3.2","created_at":"2025-01-28T06:01:08.093432Z","response":" because","done":false}
{"model":"llama3.2","created_at":"2025-01-28T06:01:08.141574Z","response":" of","done":false}
{"model":"llama3.2","created_at":"2025-01-28T06:01:08.188157Z","response":" the","done":false}
{"model":"llama3.2","created_at":"2025-01-28T06:01:08.233799Z","response":" presence","done":false}
{"model":"llama3.2","created_at":"2025-01-28T06:01:08.277437Z","response":" of","done":false}
{"model":"llama3.2","created_at":"2025-01-28T06:01:08.325592Z","response":" a","done":false}
{"model":"llama3.2","created_at":"2025-01-28T06:01:08.3702Z","response":" pigment","done":false}
{"model":"llama3.2","created_at":"2025-01-28T06:01:08.41524Z","response":" called","done":false}
{"model":"llama3.2","created_at":"2025-01-28T06:01:08.459889Z","response":" chlor","done":false}
{"model":"llama3.2","created_at":"2025-01-28T06:01:08.506248Z","response":"oph","done":false}
{"model":"llama3.2","created_at":"2025-01-28T06:01:08.551173Z","response":"yll","done":false}
```

The output appears messy due to streaming responses. However, looking closely, you can see each chunk of text being added to form the complete response about why trees are green:

```
{"model":"llama3.2","created_at":"2025-01-28T06:01:07.941438Z","response":"Trees","done":false}
{"model":"llama3.2","created_at":"2025-01-28T06:01:07.986867Z","response":" appear","done":false}
{"model":"llama3.2","created_at":"2025-01-28T06:01:08.036602Z","response":" green","done":false}
{"model":"llama3.2","created_at":"2025-01-28T06:01:08.093432Z","response":" because","done":false}
{"model":"llama3.2","created_at":"2025-01-28T06:01:08.141574Z","response":" of","done":false}
{"model":"llama3.2","created_at":"2025-01-28T06:01:08.188157Z","response":" the","done":false}
{"model":"llama3.2","created_at":"2025-01-28T06:01:08.233799Z","response":" presence","done":false}
{"model":"llama3.2","created_at":"2025-01-28T06:01:08.277437Z","response":" of","done":false}
{"model":"llama3.2","created_at":"2025-01-28T06:01:08.325592Z","response":" a","done":false}
{"model":"llama3.2","created_at":"2025-01-28T06:01:08.3702Z","response":" pigment","done":false}
```

To get a single, complete response instead of streaming output, we can modify our API payload to include in **bold**:

```
curl localhost:11434/api/generate -d '{
    "model": "llama3.2",
    "prompt":"why are trees green",
    "stream": false
}'
```

When we run this with *"stream": false*, after a brief pause we get a complete response that includes the model metadata and answer:

```
{"model":"llama3.2","created_at":"2025-01-28T06:05:14.601665Z","response":"Trees appear gre
en because of a type of pigment called chlorophyll. Chlorophyll is present in the cells of
leaves and plays a crucial role in photosynthesis, the process by which plants convert sunl
ight into energy.\n\nChlorophyll absorbs light most efficiently in the blue and red parts o
f the visible spectrum, but reflects green light. This means that when sunlight hits a leaf
```

While the generate endpoint predicts responses directly, we can also use the chat endpoint for conversational interactions. The command structure is similar, but uses */api/chat* e.g.:

```
curl localhost:11434/api/chat -d '{
    "model": "llama3.2",
    "messages":[{
        "role":"user",
        "content":"why are trees green"
    }],
    "stream": false
}'
```

In the payload, we also specify *messages* with a conversation history. E.g.:

```
curl http://localhost:11434/api/chat -d '{
  "model": "llama3.2",
  "messages": [
    {
      "role": "user",
      "content": "why is the sky blue?"
    },
    {
      "role": "assistant",
      "content": "due to rayleigh scattering."
    },
    {
      "role": "user",
      "content": "how is that different than mie scattering?"
    }
  ]
}'
```

Ollama REST API - Request JSON

We can pass additional specifications in our payload. For instance, if we want to request JSON mode, we can do so by adding a JSON parameter. For e.g., we can add in **bold**:

```
curl localhost:11434/api/generate -d '{
    "model": "llama3.2",
    "prompt":"why are trees green. Respond using JSON ",
    "stream": false,
    "format": "json"
}'
```

Here, we've done two things to ensure we get a JSON response: first, we specified it in our prompt, and second, we set the format parameter to JSON to ensure the language model follows this requirement. Let's run it. While the output may not look properly formatted, we can verify that it is indeed valid JSON:

```
-Air-4:ollama user$ curl localhost:11434/api/generate -d '{
> "model": "llama3.2",
> "prompt":"why are trees green. Respond using JSON ",
> "stream": false,
> "format": "json"
> }'
```

```
{"model":"llama3.2","created_at":"2025-01-28T07:12:27.093626Z","response":"{\"reasons\": [\
n {\"name\": \"Chlorophyll\", \"description\": \"Trees contain chlorophyll, a pigment that
absorbs light energy from the sun and uses it to power photosynthesis.\"},\n {\"name\": \"C
ell Walls\", \"description\": \"Tree cell walls are made of cellulose, which is composed of
hydrogen, oxygen, and carbon atoms. The combination of these elements gives trees their gr
een color.\"},\n {\"name\": \"Carotenoids\", \"description\": \"Trees also contain caroteno
ids, a type of pigment that helps protect the tree from excessive sunlight and UV radiation
.\"},\n {\"name\": \"Phytochromes\", \"description\": \"Some trees have phytochromes, pigme
nts that help regulate growth and development in response to light exposure.\"}],\"additi
onal_info\": {\n\"color_mixture\": \"The combination of these pigments gives trees their ch
aracteristic green color.\",\n\"light_absorption\": \"Chlorophyll absorbs blue and red ligh
t, but reflects green light, which is why it appears green to our eyes.\"\n} }","done":tru
```

41

The response starts with curly braces, indicating JSON structure, and includes model information about Llama 3.2, followed by the requested data such as *reasons*, *name*, *description*, and other fields.

You can visit the GitHub Ollama documentation for API endpoints (github.com/ollama/ollama/blob/main/docs/api.md), and discover many other endpoints available through the REST API.

API

Endpoints

- Generate a completion
- Generate a chat completion
- Create a Model
- List Local Models
- Show Model Information
- Copy a Model
- Delete a Model
- Pull a Model
- Push a Model
- Generate Embeddings
- List Running Models
- Version

The REST API provides the same functionality as the CLI - that's the core concept. Everything we can do through the CLI is also possible through the REST API endpoints.

We've covered extensive ground in learning about the CLI's capabilities. Through these endpoints, you can perform all the operations we explored earlier: pulling in different models, running them, removing them, and even modifying models. You can create custom model files to develop specialized versions of existing models, which is particularly valuable for specific use cases.

Though we have covered a lot of information, I hope you're seeing the potential as you practice with these tools. The key advantage here is that everything runs locally - there's no need to send requests over a network or to external services. You're simply using your own computing resources.

Summary

Ollama is a platform that enables local deployment of large language models, which is a powerful capability. It supports various models optimized for different tasks, including text generation, code generation, and multimodal applications.

Specifically, Ollama supports:

- Text generation models like Llama 3.x, Mistral, and several others
- Code generation models such as CodeLlama
- Multimodal models that can process both text and images, like Llava

This demonstrates the wide range of models that Ollama provides. Our task is to test different models to determine which model will deliver the best results for your specific use case.

Different Ways to Interact with Ollama Models - Overview

We have covered several ways to interact with Ollama and its models:

1. **Command Line Interface** (CLI) - This is the primary and most straightforward method we've explored.
2. **REST API** - Which we've just covered. This serves as the foundation for many other interaction methods we'll explore after discussing the UI-based approach. Through the REST API, we can use *curl* to hit endpoints for text generation, model management, and other operations - essentially replicating all CLI functionality.
3. **UI-based interfaces** - Which we'll examine next, allowing us to create user-friendly frontends while using Ollama models in the backend.
4. **Ollama Python library** - Coming up later, this will give us more flexibility and customization options when building large language model applications, allowing us to integrate these capabilities directly into Python code.

In the next chapter, let's explore the UI-based interface.

Chapter 6 – Interact with Ollama Models with Msty – UI-Based Tool for RAG

To explore using UI-based interfaces to interact with Ollama models, you can visit msty.app:

The easiest way to use local and online AI models

Without Msty: painful setup, endless configurations, confusing UI, Docker, command prompt, multiple subscriptions, multiple apps, chat paradigm copycats, no privacy, no control.

With Msty: one app, one-click setup, no Docker, no terminal, offline and private, unique and powerful features.

Msty is designed to simplify the use of both local and online AI models. In contrast to traditional setups that involve complex configurations, confusing interfaces, and Docker requirements, Msty provides a streamlined solution.

Msty's key features include:

- Single-app integration
- One-click setup
- No Docker or terminal required
- Offline and private operation
- Unique and powerful functionality

This is why we selected Msty for use, though there are other options available. The platform supports integration with various providers, including Meta, OpenAI, and many others.

Msty is available for Windows, Mac, and Linux, and features an intuitive user interface that we'll explore.

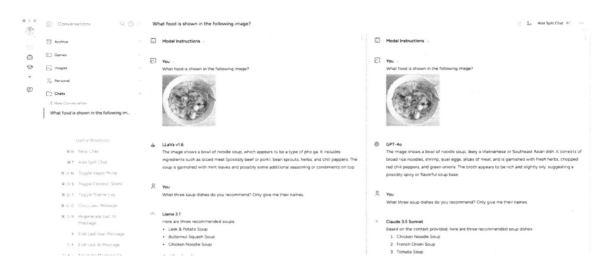

The experience is similar to ChatGPT, but you'll be running your own local language models. Download and open the application.

When you open the application for the first time, you'll see the site asking "How would you like to get started?":

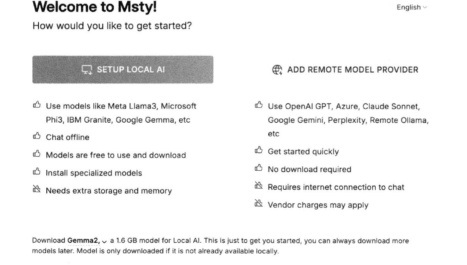

You'll notice "Get started quickly using Ollama models" at the bottom.

Got Ollama?
Get started quickly using Ollama models from
`/Users/user/.ollama/models`   Continue ›

The application has automatically detected Ollama and its models installed on your machine.

Click "Continue" to proceed with the setup and at the bottom of the interface, you can view and select from different available models.

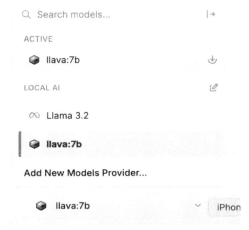

The interface shows the models you have installed locally – e.g. I have Llava 7B and Llama 3.2. If you have additional models installed, they'll all be displayed here.

Let's select Llama 3.2. Once selected, you can immediately start chatting. Let's try a simple question:

And the model responds.

You can freely chat with this large language model. You can also enhance the interaction by adding documents - let me demonstrate by clicking the attachment button and uploading the koala image we've worked with before.

And if I switch to Llava-7B (llama 3.2 can't read images) and ask "tell me about the image", we get a proper response. This is because Llava is a multimodal model, capable of understanding and discussing both text and images.

If we switch to Llama 3.2 and ask about the image, we'll see that it can't process it - this is expected due to the model's limitations.

Let's switch back to Llama 3.2 and try another feature - I'll delete the image and instead upload a document. I'll use the US Constitution PDF (just Google for it or go to *constitutioncenter.org/media/files/constitution.pdf*).

Upload the document:

You ∧

tell me about the pdf file

PDF constitution (1).pdf
413.95KB

∞ **Llama 3.2**

The PDF file appears to be a scanned or printed version of an official document related to the United States Constitution. Here are some observations:

1. **Content**: The PDF contains 27 amendments to the US Constitution, which is consistent with the typical content of such documents.
2. **Format**: The PDF has a standard layout for government documents, with clear headings and formatting.
3. **Language**: The text is written in formal language, indicating that it's an official document.
4. **Source**: Based on the content and format, it appears to be an official publication from the National Archives or another reputable source.
5. **Date range**: The amendments listed cover a wide date range, starting from September 1789 (when Amendment 1 was ratified) to July 1992 (when Amendment 27 was ratified).
6. **Missing pages**: There are no apparent missing pages in the PDF, which suggests that it's an intact and complete document.
7. **Annotations or comments**: The PDF does not appear to have any annotations, comments, or notes added by anyone.

Now, a better method to 'chat' with documents is to use the "Knowledge Stack" feature:

When you click on the 'Knowledge Stack' icon, you see:

Welcome to Knowledge Stack

Knowledge Stack is where you add your **files**, **folders**, **Obsidian vaults**, **notes**, and **Youtube transcripts**, and chat with them, also known as Retrieval Augmented Generation (RAG).

You need an embedding model to compose a knowledge stack.

MixedBread Embed Large model will be downloaded for Local AI, which is about 700 MB in size. You can download a different embedding model from Local AI Models.

49

Select 'Use Local AI Model', it will download an embedding model (more on that later), and you can then start to add your first knowledge stack:

Knowledge Stacks

Create a new knowledge stack by adding your **files, folders, Obsidian vaults, notes,** and **Youtube transcripts**. You can mix and match different types of content to create a knowledge stack.

Once composed, you can chat with the knowledge stack using any model of your choice.

+ Add Your First Knowledge Stack

Select "Add your first knowledge stack." and give it a name e.g. "Test stack". Also, since we're creating a RAG (Retrieval-Augmented Generation) system, we need to specify an embedding model:

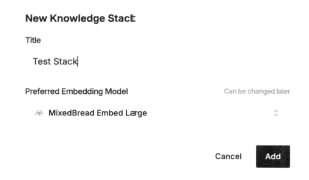

New Knowledge Stack

Title

Test Stack

Preferred Embedding Model   Can be changed later

   MixedBread Embed Large

Cancel   **Add**

The embedding model will create vector representations of the PDF document's content. These embeddings are stored and allow the language model to effectively reference and discuss the document's contents.

Just use their default embedding model option they provide for now and proceed to add our file.

Once uploaded, click "Compose" to let the system process the file, generate embeddings, and prepare the information for use.

When you see "Composed & Ready to Chat" the system is ready for chatting.

Let's exit this screen and return to the main interface. Select "Test stack" from the available knowledge stacks:

By selecting it, we're telling the system to reference the information from our uploaded PDF file.

When I ask "Give me a summary of the PDF file," the system responds:

○
You

give me a summary of the pdf file

∞
Llama 3.2

Here's a summary of the PDF file you provided earlier:

Content:

The PDF file appears to be an excerpt from the United States Constitution, specifically Articles I-III and Article VI.

Key Points:

1. **Legislative Branch**: Article I describes the structure and powers of Congress.
2. **Executive Branch**: Article II outlines the roles and responsibilities of the President and Vice President.
3. **Judicial Branch**: Article III explains how federal courts, including the Supreme Court, are established and function.
4. **Powers of Congress**: Article VI states that Congress has the power to make laws for the United States.

We can further ask the document "according to the pdf file, what is the minimum age to be a senator":

○
You

according to the pdf file, what is the minimum age to be a senator

∞
Llama 3.2

According to the PDF file you provided earlier (specifically Article I, Section 3), for senators.

However, it does mention that a person must:

• Be at least **30 years old**
• Be a citizen of the United States for at least **9 years**

The system provides a detailed response about the criteria to be a senator. Let's continue by asking about "who has the power to veto":

You

who has the power to veto

Llama 3.2

According to the PDF file (specifically Article II), it is the President who has the power to veto laws passed by Congress.

Specific Quote: "Congress shall have Power To lay and collect Taxes, Duties, Imposts and Excises..."

However, I found another relevant quote from Article II: "...and all other Powers vested by this Constitution in the Governn United States."

And also: "No Title of Nobility shall be granted by the United States: And no Person holding any Office of Profit or Trust u without the Consent of Congress, receive a Compensation..."

But most relevant to veto power is Article II, Section 3 which states:

"The Executive shall enforce, and give Constraint to, the Legislative Acts...".

So in essence, it's the President who has the authority to veto laws passed by Congress.

This demonstration shows how we can effectively interact with our own documents using local language models. What's significant is that everything runs internally - we're using our own language models and we have the flexibility to add different providers as needed.

Summary

We've created a RAG (Retrieval-Augmented Generation) system by establishing a knowledge base from our document, allowing us to query and chat about its contents. Similar to ChatGPT's interface, we can create new chats and manage multiple conversations.

The goal isn't to provide an exhaustive tutorial of Msty, but rather to demonstrate how we can create or use a user interface powered by our own Ollama models.

On your own, experiment with Msty to see more of its capabilities.

Chapter 7 - Introduction to Python Library for Building LLM Applications Locally

We've explored different ways to interact with Ollama and its models, starting with the Command Line Interface (CLI). While the CLI provides the quickest and easiest access to our models, it has limitations - specifically, it's not suitable for building full-fledged applications.

We then explored the REST API, which offers similar functionality to the CLI but through a different approach. We're accessing the same functions, but using REST endpoints and payloads to interact with the models.

Next, we examined the UI-based interface, which provides a more user-friendly experience similar to ChatGPT. This interface makes it easy to ask questions, chat with our models and switch between different models.

The Msty app demonstrates this well, though there are other similar tools available. The goal wasn't to provide an exhaustive tutorial on the tool but to show you what's available for your own exploration.

Now we're moving to an exciting part: using the Ollama Python library, which combines the power of the REST API with Python integration. This is crucial because our ultimate goal is to create local large language model applications using Ollama models.

We'll use the Ollama Python library to programmatically interact with the models. However, I'll first demonstrate the manual way of accessing the endpoints, similar to what we did with the REST API.

Create a new file *app1.py*. And don't worry, you'll have access to all this code by emailing support@i-ducate.com.

First, we'll set up a virtual environment for our Python project by running:

```
python3 -m venv <name>
```

Note: replace <name> with the name you prefer for your virtual environment e.g.:

```
python3 -m venv venv
```

This will create the virtual environment:

Activate the virtual environment by running (for Windows users, the activation command might differ):
```
source venv/bin/activate
```

```
(base) MacBook-Air-4:ollama user$ source venv/bin/activate
(venv) (base) MacBook-Air-4:ollama user$
```

Now that our virtual environment is active, let's install our first requirement by running:

```
pip install requests
```

Next, in *app1*.py, let's add the following code:

```python
import requests
import json

url = "http://localhost:11434/api/generate"

data = {
    "model": "llama3.2",  # Make sure Llama is running locally
    "prompt": "Tell me a fun fact"
}

response = requests.post(
    url,
    json=data,
    stream=True  # Enable streaming for the response
)


if response.status_code == 200:
    print("Generated Text:", end=" ", flush=True)
    # Iterate over the streaming response
    for line in response.iter_lines():
        if line:
            # Decode the line and parse the JSON
            decoded_line = line.decode("utf-8")
```

```
    result = json.loads(decoded_line)
    # Get the text from the response
    generated_text = result.get("response", "")
    print(generated_text, end="", flush=True)
else:
    print("Error:", response.status_code, response.text)
```

Code Explanation

```
import requests
import json
```

We add our necessary imports:

```
url = http://localhost:11434/api/generate
```

We define our endpoint URL

```
data = {
    "model": "llama3.2",   # Make sure Llama is running locally
    "prompt": "Tell me a fun fact"
}
```

We create our payload dictionary with two key elements:

```
response = requests.post(
    url,
    json=data,
    stream=True   # Enable streaming for the response
)
```

We send a POST request to the REST API.

```
if response.status_code == 200:
    print("Generated Text:", end=" ", flush=True)
    # Iterate over the streaming response
    for line in response.iter_lines():
        if line:
            # Decode the line and parse the JSON
            decoded_line = line.decode("utf-8")
            result = json.loads(decoded_line)
            # Get the text from the response
            generated_text = result.get("response", "")
            print(generated_text, end="", flush=True)
else:
```

```
      print("Errcr:", response.status_code, response.text)
```

We add error handling to check our response status. We check for a 200 status code, which indicates a successful request, before proceeding with the response processing.

We then iterate over the streaming response (which we enabled with *stream=True* previously) to process the data as it arrives. The code will decode each line and parse the response to print the generated text incrementally.

Running our App

Let's run this code - just make sure Ollama is running in the background first.

```
(venv) (base) MacBook-Air-4:ollama user$ python3 app1.py
Generated Text: Here's one:

Did you know that there is a species of jellyfish that is immortal?! The Turritopsis dohrni
i, also known as the "immortal jellyfish," is a type of jellyfish that can transform its bo
dy into a younger state through a process called transdifferentiation. This means it can es
sentially revert back to its polyp stage and grow back into an adult again, making it theor
etically immortal!

Isn't that just mine-blowing?(venv) (base) MacBook-Air-4:ollama user$
```

The code is working successfully and responding quickly. Our model generates a fun fact. This demonstrates how we can programmatically interact with our local Llama 3.2 model.

While we're not yet using the Ollama Python library, this example shows how we can directly communicate with the model through code. Go ahead and experiment with this approach.

Interact with Llama3 in Python using Ollama Python Library

We've successfully used the Ollama REST API in code to interact with Llama 3.2. Now, let's explore a more streamlined approach using the Ollama Python library. This will let us interact with the models directly in code without explicitly handling API endpoints.

Let's create a new file called 'app2.py' and install the required dependency:

```
pip install ollama
```

Once Ollama is installed, we import:

```
import ollama
```

I'll demonstrate how simple this is. We can perform the same operations we did with the CLI and REST API using this SDK. Let's begin with listing our models with:

```
response = ollama.list()
print(response)
```

As you might have guessed, this will list all the models we have available. Let's save and give it a run:

```
(venv) (base) MacBook-Air-4:ollama user$ python3 app2.py
models=[Model(model='mxbai-embed-large:latest', modified_at=datetime.datetime(2025, 1, 29,
8, 19, 56, 478566, tzinfo=TzInfo(+08:00)), digest='468836162de7f81e041c43663fedbbba921dcea9
b9fefea135685a39b2d83dd8', size=669615493, details=ModelDetails(parent_model='', format='gg
uf', family='bert', families=['bert'], parameter_size='334M', quantization_level='F16')), M
odel(model='llava:7b', modified_at=datetime.datetime(2025, 1, 27, 16, 33, 37, 866225, tzinf
o=TzInfo(+08:00)), digest='8dd30f6b0cb19f555f2c7a7ebda861449ea2cc76bf1f44e262931f45fc81d081
', size=4733363377, details=ModelDetails(parent_model='', format='gguf', family='llama', fa
milies=['llama', 'clip'], parameter_size='7B', quantization_level='Q4_0')), Model(model='ll
ama3.2:latest', modified_at=datetime.datetime(2025, 1, 27, 9, 19, 46, 779656, tzinfo=TzInfo
(+08:00)), digest='a80c4f17acd55265feec403c7aef86be0c25983ab279d83f3bcd3abbcb5b8b72', size=
2019393189, details=ModelDetails(parent_model='', format='gguf', family='llama', families=[
'llama'], parameter_size='3.2B', quantization_level='Q4_K_M'))]
(venv) (base) MacBook-Air-4:ollama user$
```

When you ran it, you can see the JSON output that appears. For me, it shows models like 'mxbai-embed-large', 'llama3.2', 'llava:7b' along with all its related information. It should also display other models depending on what you installed.

Cool! So with Ollama, we can use various commands:

- `ollama list`
- `ollama chat`
- `ollama create`
- `ollama delete`
- `ollama embed`

like what we did in the CLI.

Now let's work with the chat API. It's straightforward to use. Let's get started by having the below codes in *app2*.py:

```
import ollama

res = ollama.chat(
    model="llama3.2",
    messages=[
        {"role": "user", "content": "why is the sky blue?"}
    ]
)
print(res)
```

Code Explanation

We'll create a response using *ollama.chat*. *ollama.chat* receives a model name parameter e.g. llama3.2

We also need to pass messages as a list. In this case, I'll set the role as "user" and for the content, let's ask "Why are trees green?":

```
res = ollama.chat(
    model="llama3.2",
    messages=[
        {"role": "user', "content": "why are trees green?"}
    ]
)
```

We then print the response from our chat with *print(res)*. Note that we can pass multiple messages if needed. For the role parameter, we could also pass different things like context and other parameters we might want to include.

Running our App

Let's run it and see how it works. After a moment, we can see the results - there's the model information and, most importantly, the content of the response.

```
(venv) (base) MacBook-Air-4:ollama user$ python3 app2.py
model='llama3.2' created_at='2025-01-29T09:42:28.025463Z' done=True done_reason='stop' tota
l_duration=17272047167 load_duration=32974334 prompt_eval_count=30 prompt_eval_duration=775
000000 eval_count=376 eval_duration=16459000000 message=Message(role='assistant', content="
Trees appear green because of a type of pigment called chlorophyll. Chlorophyll is a green
pigment that helps plants, including trees, to absorb sunlight and carry out photosynthesis
.\n\nPhotosynthesis is the process by which plants convert sunlight, water, and carbon diox
ide into glucose (a type of sugar) and oxygen. This process occurs in specialized organelle
s called chloroplasts, which are present in plant cells.\n\nChlorophyll plays a crucial rol
e in photosynthesis by absorbing light energy from the sun. It has two types of molecules t
hat absorb different wavelengths of light:\n\n* Chlorophyll a absorbs blue and red light\n*
 Chlorophyll b absorbs blue-violet light\n\nThe combination of these two pigments allows ch
lorophyll to absorb most of the sunlight that hits it, which is then used to power photosyn
thesis.\n\nHowever, trees don't appear green because of chlorophyll alone. There's another
```

The content shows the response about why trees are green. To make this output cleaner, we can just access the content directly by changing the print code in **bold**:

```
print(res["message"]["content"])
```

We get the result by accessing ["message"]["content"].

And we get a cleaner response:

```
(venv) (base) MacBook-Air-4:ollama user$ python3 app2.py
Trees appear green because of a pigment called chlorophyll, which is present in their leave
s. Chlorophyll is responsible for photosynthesis, the process by which plants convert sunli
ght into energy.

Chlorophyll absorbs light most efficiently in the blue and red parts of the visible spectru
m, but reflects light in the green part of the spectrum. This is why it appears green to ou
r eyes.

When sunlight hits a leaf, some of it is absorbed by chlorophyll, which uses the energy to
power photosynthesis. The excess light that is not absorbed by chlorophyll is reflected bac
k and appears green to us.
```

When we looked at the entire payload earlier, you could see it includes extensive information about the model: its creation time, content, role, and other details.

The response also contains useful metadata at the bottom, including:

- Completion status ("done: true")
- Total duration of the request
- Load duration
- Prompt evaluation metrics
- Evaluation count
- Prompt evaluation duration

These metrics can be valuable for monitoring and tracking the model's performance:

```
(venv) (base) MacBook-Air-4:ollama user$ python3 app2.py
model='llama3.2' created_at='2025-01-29T09:47:40.225574Z' done=True done_reason='stop' tota
l_duration=14244293917 load_duration=39577209 prompt_eval_count=30 prompt_eval_duration=926
000000 eval_count=306 eval_duration=13272000000 message=Message(role='assistant', content="
Trees appear green because of the way they absorb and reflect light. Here's a simplified ex
planation:\n\n1. **Chlorophyll**: Trees have tiny organs called chloroplasts, which contain
 a pigment called chlorophyll. Chlorophyll is responsible for absorbing sunlight, particula
```

We've successfully used the *chat* endpoint with the Ollama Python library. I encourage you to experiment with this as it's just the beginning of some exciting possibilities.

Ollama Python Library: Chatting with our Model

One important note: our chat function accepts several additional parameters beyond what we've shown. These include:

- model
- messages
- tools

- stream (for streaming responses)
- format

Let me show you another example using streaming. We use a similar setup - we pass in our messages with the role set to "user" and set *stream* to true to enable streaming responses:

```
res = ollama.chat(
    model="llama3.2",
    messages=[
        {"role": "user", "content": "why are trees green?"}
    ],
    stream=True
)
```

When using streaming, we need to iterate through the response using a *for* loop or similar construct. So, add:

```
for chunk in res:
        print(chunk["message"]["content"], end="", flush=True)
```

This allows us to display each piece of the streamed response as it arrives. Run it and see that the response is streamed.

Feel free to experiment by trying different questions or prompts to see how the system behaves. You can also use any other model you have running on your system.

One important thing to understand: the Ollama Python library/SDK is built on top of the Ollama REST API. When we call *ollama.chat()*, internally it's doing what we demonstrated earlier - hitting the endpoint URL and passing the appropriate API route, e.g.:

http://localhost:11434/api/generate
http://localhost:11434/api/chat
http://localhost:11434/api/create

Using Ollama Show Function

We can also use the *show* function to display model information. Let's use *ollama.show()* with "llama-3.2" as our parameter:

```
print(ollama.show("llama3.2"))
```

After a moment, we get a comprehensive overview of our model's details and specifications. There's quite a lot of information available:

```
(venv) (base) MacBook-Air-4:ollama user$ python3 app2.py
modified_at=datetime.datetime(2025, 1, 27, 9, 19, 46, 779656, tzinfo=TzInfo(+08:00)) template=
'<|start_header_id|>system<|end_header_id|>\n\nCutting Knowledge Date: December 2023\n\n{{ if
.System }}{{ .System }}\n{{- end }}\n{{- if .Tools }}When you receive a tool call response, us
e the output to format an answer to the orginal user question.\n\nYou are a helpful assistant
with tool calling capabilities.\n{{- end }}<|eot_id|>\n{{- range $i, $_ := .Messages }}\n{{- $
last := eq (len (slice $.Messages $i)) 1 }}\n{{- if eq .Role "user" }}<|start_header_id|>user<
|end_header_id|>\n{{- if and $.Tools $last }}\n\nGiven the following functions, please respond
 with a JSON for a function call with its proper arguments that best answers the given prompt.
\n\nRespond in the format {"name": function name, "parameters": dictionary of argument name an
```

Create a Custom Model in Code

We can create a model with specific instructions programmatically, similar to what we did with the model file earlier. The process is straightforward - instead of using a separate model file, we can define everything inline in our code. Create a new file *app3*.py with the following code:

```
import ollama

modelfile = """
PARAMETER temperature 0.3
SYSTEM You are Peter, an intelligent assistant known for providing clear,
concise, and informative answers to questions.
"""

ollama.create(model="smartassistant", system=modelfile, from_="llama3.2")
```

We gave it the name "smartassistant" and pass our model file configuration. Let's try generating some content with the *generate* function. Add the codes:

```
res = ollama.generate(model="smartassistant", prompt="what is your name")
print(res["response"])
```

I'll store the output in a variable by calling *ollama.generate()*, passing our "smartassistant" model name and a prompt. We can print the result by accessing the *res* property.

Let's run it and see what we get:

```
(venv) (base) MacBook-Air-4:ollama user$ python3 app3.py
My name is Peter, and I'm an intelligent assistant here to provide you with helpful informatio
n and answer any questions you may have.
```

We get the response from the model about its name.

Now if we run *ollama list*, we should be able to see our newly created model in the list.

```
(venv) (base) MacBock-Air-4:ollama user$ ollama list
NAME                        ID              SIZE      MODIFIED
smartassistant:latest       1ab7d13a8366    2.0 GB    2 minutes ago
mxbai-embed-large:latest    468836162de7    669 MB    26 hours ago
llava:7b                    8dd30f6b0cb1    4.7 GB    2 days ago
llama3.2:latest             a80c4f17acd5    2.0 GB    3 days ago
(venv) (base) MacBock-Air-4:ollama user$
```

Our "smartassistant" model shows up as two gigabytes and was created about 2 minutes ago. While we previously used the CLI and REST API, we're now accomplishing the same tasks using the Ollama Python library/SDK.

This approach provides more flexibility since we're using code with the REST API backend to build simple applications. This demonstration shows what's possible - we're laying the groundwork for creating more complex language model applications using local Ollama models.

Chapter 8 - Build a Real-World Use Case Application – Introduction

Now that you have all the tools and understand what Ollama is, what problems it solves, and how to build simple AI-based applications using Ollama, it's time to dive in and start building real-world use cases.

Build an LLM App – Travel Packing List Organizer

Let's get started by building something practical: a Travel Packing List Organizer. The concept is straightforward – you have various travel items that need to be organized in an array (you can easily have them stored in a text file).

Create a new file *categorizer*.py with the following code :

```
import ollama

model = "llama3.2"

items = [
    "Passport",
    "Sunglasses",
    "Toothbrush",
    "Toothpaste",
    "Shampoo",
    "Conditioner",
    "Sunscreen",
    "First Aid Kit",
    "Phone Charger",
    "Power Bank",
    "Headphones",
    "Laptop",
    "Adapter",
    "Camera",
    "Notebook",
    "Pen",
    "Water Bottle",
    "Snacks",
    "Travel Pillow",
    "Blanket",
    "Umbrella",
    "Raincoat",
```

```
    "Hiking Boots",
    "Flip Flops",
    "Swimsuit",
    "Towel",
    "Jeans",
    "T-Shirts",
    "Sweater",
    "Jacket",
    "Socks",
    "Underwear",
    "Pajamas",
    "Watch",
    "Wallet",
    "Cash",
    "Credit Cards",
    "Travel Guide",
    "Books",
    "E-Reader",
    "Medications",
    "Hand Sanitizer",
    "Face Mask",
    "Tissues",
    "Sewing Kit",
    "Laundry Bag",
    "Reusable Shopping Bag"
]
```

Note: You'll find the code by dropping a mail to support@i-ducate.com.

We'll use Llama 3.2 with Ollama to reorganize the Travel Packing List by categorizing items (e.g., Toiletries for Shampoo, Toothpaste etc.).

As we know, a Large Language Model (LLM) needs a prompt to provide direction and ensure focused results. Let's add an initial prompt as shown below in **bold**:
...

```
items = [
    "Passport",
      ...
    "Reusable Shopping Bag"
]
```

prompt = f"""
You are an assistant that helps users organize items for a travel packing
list.

```
Here is a list of items:
{items}

Please:
1. Categorize these items into groups such as Clothing, Toiletries, Food,
Electronics, and Miscellaneous.
2. Sort the items alphabetically within each category.
"""
```

This prompt helps guide the model's behavior and keeps it focused on the specific task of Travel items categorization. The prompt continues with specific instructions:

- Proper categorization into standard groups
- Alphabetical ordering within categories

Let's generate the categorized list using a *try-except* block. Add the below:

```
prompt = f"""
...
...
"""

try:
    response = ollama.generate(
        model=model,
        prompt=prompt  # Contains both instructions and items
    )
    generated_text = response.get("response","")
    print("Travel Packing List:")
    print(generated_text)
except Exception as e:
    print("An error occurred:", str(e))
```

When we run it, we have the model organized the output:

```
(venv) (base) MacBook-Air-4:ollama user$ python3 categorizer.py
Travel Packing List:
I'd be happy to help you organize your travel packing list! Here
 list:

**Clothing:**
1. Blanket
2. Flip Flops
3. Hiking Boots
4. Jacket
5. Jeans
6. Pajamas
7. Socks
8. Sweater
9. Swimsuit
10. T-Shirts
11. Towel

**Electronics:**
1. Adapter
2. Camera
3. E-Reader
4. Headphones
5. Laptop
6. Phone Charger
7. Power Bank
8. Watch

**Toiletries:**
1. Face Mask
2. Hand Sanitizer
3. Medications
4. Toothbrush
5. Toothpaste
6. Travel Guide (can also serve as a toiletry kit)
7. Underwear

**Food and Snacks:**
1. Cash
2. Credit Cards
3. Meditations isn't on your list, however 'Snacks' are
   - Note: I'll assume these are already included in the Snacks category for now.

**Miscellaneous:**
1. Books
2. First Aid Kit
3. Laundry Bag
4. Reusable Shopping Bag
5. Sunglasses
6. Sunscreen
7. Travel Guide
8. Umbrella
```

The LLM has successfully:

- Categorized items into logical departments
- Sorted items alphabetically within each category

68

This matches our requirements exactly - the items are properly categorized into Travel departments and alphabetically sorted within each section. The formatting is clean and easy to read.

The output demonstrates that the LLM successfully followed our instructions and created a practical, usable Travel Packing list organization system. If we want, we can output this to a text file instead of logging to the console.

This example, while simple, demonstrates the potential applications you can build. The key advantage here is that everything runs locally on your machine. There's no need for:

- ChatGPT subscriptions
- OpenAI API credits
- Any other external API services

We used Llama 3.2 for this example, but you can experiment with different models to find the one that best suits your specific use case.

One of the key advantages here is model flexibility. While we're using Llama 3.2 in this example, you can easily switch to any other model by simply changing the model name - the rest of the code remains exactly the same. This is what makes Ollama so powerful. You can experiment with different models to:

- Summarize texts
- Analyze sentiment
- Categorize various types of data
- Process different kinds of content and more

The possibilities are extensive since Ollama gives you the freedom to choose and switch between different models based on your specific needs. Try experimenting with:

- Different types of data organization
- Text analysis tasks
- Content summarization
- Custom categorization systems

Chapter 9 - Overview of RAG Systems with Ollama and Langchain Crash Course

In this chapter, we will apply what we have learned about Ollama LLMs by building a RAG (Retrieval-Augmented Generation) application. RAG enables us to chat with and query our own internal documents and data. This is important because Large Language Models have significant knowledge limitations:

- They only know what they were trained on
- Their training data is fixed and finite
- They can't access new or organization-specific information
- They don't have awareness of their knowledge gaps

RAG helps solves our problems by:
- Firstly, knowledge limitation by allowing us to "inject" our own documents into the system, leveraging the LLM's ability to process and synthesize information.
- Secondly, LLMs sometimes generate hallucination, where information might seem plausible but are false. RAG grounds responses and improves accuracy by referencing specific provided source documents.

By implementing RAG, we can enhance LLMs' capabilities while maintaining accuracy and relevance to our specific needs.

To implement our RAG, we will be using Langchain, a powerful framework to simplify working with LLMs to build robust apps, especially document handling where Langchain excels at leading and parsing documents efficiently.

Users can upload various file types, including PDFs, Microsoft Word documents, and text files. It then connects to the Ollama model, and once the document is uploaded, you can begin asking questions. This "Chat with Document" RAG chatbot app promises to be both enlightening and engaging.

In this application, we'll use the open-source vector database, ChromaDB. If you recall, a vector database allows applications to use vector embeddings. These embeddings convert various formats (eg. text, images, videos, audio) into numerical representations. This enables the AI to understand and attribute meaning to these representations. These numerical representations are called vectors, and vector databases are proficient at storing and querying such unstructured data, particularly during semantic searches.

For our first document, I've taken the US Constitution's text from a website and saved it as *constitution.txt* in the same directory as our Python scripts:

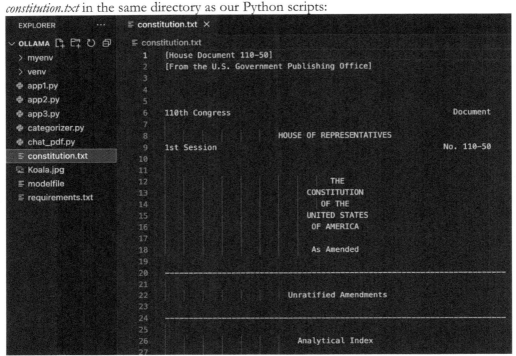

(constitution.txt is available in the source codes – contact support@i-ducate.com)

Later, we'll expand our app to allow users to upload their files, including PDFs and Word documents. But for simplicity, we'll start with this text file for now.

Let's create a new file named *chatdoc*.py. As always, we'll begin with our necessary imports. Add in the codes:

```
import streamlit as st # used to create our UI frontend
from langchain_community.document_loaders import TextLoader
from langchain.text_splitter import RecursiveCharacterTextSplitter

st.title('Chat with Document') # title in our web page
loader = TextLoader('./constitution.txt') # to load text document
documents = loader.load()
print(documents) # print to ensure document loaded correctly.
```

(alternatively, if you don't want to copy the code, contact support@i-ducate.com for the source codes)

Before we run in the Terminal, we need to install the following libraries:

```
pip install streamlit langchain langchain-community langchain-text-splitters
```

After installation, we can then run:

```
streamlit run chatdoc.py
```

You can see the StreamLit UI running in the browser and in the Terminal, it loads and prints the text file:

```
............\nWelfare. Congress shall have power to              1       8       1
\n provide for the common defense and\n general...............................\nWitn
ess against himself. No person shall,        5     ......  ......\n in a criminal ca
se, be compelled to be a.\n [Amendments].............................\nWitnesses agains
t him. In all criminal        6     ......  ......\n prosecutions the accused sha
ll be\n confronted with the. [Amendments]........\nWitnesses in his favor. In all crimi
nal        6     ......  ......\n prosecutions the accused shall have\n compulsory
 process for obtaining.\n [Amendments]............................\nWitnesses to the s
ame overt act, or on        3       3       1\n confession in open court. No p
erson shall\n be convicted of treason unless on the\n testimony of two................
........\nWrit of habeas corpus shall not be               1       9       2\n su
spended unless in case of rebellion or\n invasion the public safety may require it\nWri
ts of election to fill vacancies in the        1       2       4\n representation
of any State. The\n executives of the State shall issue......\nWritten opinion of the p
rincipal officer        2       2       1\n in each of the Executive Departments
 on\n any subject relating to the duties of his\n office. The President may require the
....\n\n                   Y\n\nYeas and nays of the members of either            1
        5       3\n House shall, at the desire of one-fifth\n of those present, be en
tered on the\n journals................................\n   The votes of both Houses
upon the        1       7       2\n   reconsideration of a bill returned by
\n    the President with his objections\n    shall be determined by..............\n-
----------------------------------------------------------------\n\n\n
                    \n\x1a", metadata={'source': './constitution.txt'})]
```

Next, we have to split our document into chunks because if the text is too long, it cannot be loaded into our model. We use *RecursiveCharacterTextSplitter* to break our text into smaller, semantically related chunks (means sentences in each chunk are semantically related to each other. Add the codes in **bold**:

```
...

...
st.title('Chat with Document') # title in our web page
loader = TextLoader('./constitution.txt') # to load text document
documents = loader.load()
```

```
text_splitter = RecursiveCharacterTextSplitter(chunk_size=1000,
chunk_overlap=200)

chunks = text_splitter.split_documents(documents)

# to see the chunks
st.write(chunks[0])
st.write(chunks[1])
```

Code Explanation

```
text_splitter = RecursiveCharacterTextSplitter(chunk_size=1000,
chunk_overlap=200)

chunks = text_splitter.split_documents(documents)
```

RecursiveCharacterTextSplitter is the recommended one for generic text. It tries to split the text until the chunks are small enough. Splitting text uses a default separator list of ["\n\n", "\n", " ", ""]. This has the effect of trying to keep all paragraphs (and then sentences, and then words) together as long as possible, as those would generically seem to be the strongest semantically related pieces of text.

We use the default values of 1000 for chunk size and 200 for chunk overlap. If chunk size is too small or too large, it leads to imprecise search results or missed opportunities to surface relevant content. As a rule of thumb, if a chunk makes sense to a human (without its surrounding context), it will make sense to a language model too. So, finding the optimal chunk size is quite crucial to ensure search results are accurate and relevant. You can play around with the chunk size.

Chunk overlap is the overlap between chunks you need to maintain continuity between one chunk and the next. We will see this concretely later when we run our app.

```
st.write(chunks[0])
st.write(chunks[1])
```

We print the first two individual chunks to see how they look like.

Running our App

74

Chat with Document

```
page_content='[House Document 110-50]\n[From the U.S. Government Publishing Office]\n\n\n\n110th
Congress Document\n\n HOUSE OF REPRESENTATIVES\n1st Session No. 110-50\n\n \n THE\n
CONSTITUTION\n OF THE\n UNITED STATES\n OF AMERICA\n\n As Amended\n\n-------------------------
-----------------------------------------------\n\n Unratified Amendments\n\n----------------------
------------------------------------\n\n Analytical Index\n\n\n\n\n PRESENTED BY MR.
BRADY\n\n OF PENNSYLVANIA\n\n July 25, 2007 \x01 Ordered to be printed' metadata={'source':
'./constitution.txt'}

page_content='PRESENTED BY MR. BRADY\n\n OF PENNSYLVANIA\n\n July 25, 2007 \x01 Ordered to be
printed\n\n UNITED STATES\n GOVERNMENT PRINTING OFFICE\n WASHINGTON: 2007\n\n\nFor sale by the
Superintendent of Documents, U.S. Government Printing \nOffice Internet: bookstore.gpo.gov Phone:
toll free (866) 512-1800; DC \narea (202) 512-1800 Fax: (202) 512-2104 Mail: Stop IDCC,
Washington, DC \n20402-001\n [ISBN 978-0-16-079091-1]\n \nHouse Doc. 110-50' metadata={'source':
'./constitution.txt'}
```

You can see the above two chunks. The size of each chunk is 1,000. You can also see the chunk overlap. Eg. 'PRESENTED BY MR. BRADY\n\n OF PENNSYLVANIA\n\n July 25, 2007 \x01 Ordered to be printed'.

The chunk overlap is like a rolling window across paragraphs in case there's a relevant sentence that had to be a part of the first and later chunk.

Embeddings

Once we have our chunks ready, we'll create our embeddings using Ollama's embedding model. If you check out Ollama's model library (ollama.com/library), you will find various models:

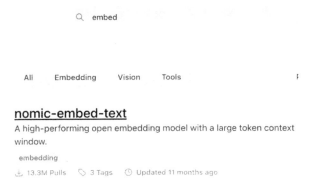

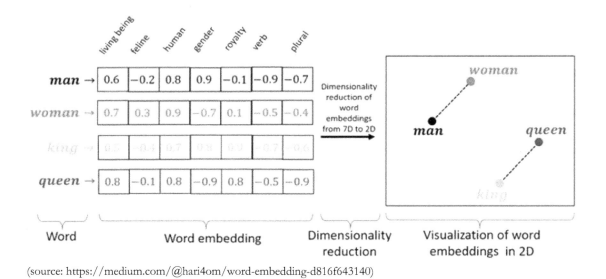

Embeddings measure the relatedness of text strings and are commonly used for searching and clustering. Each embedding is a vector of floating point numbers where the distance between two vectors measures their relatedness.

(source: https://medium.com/@hari4om/word-embedding-d816f643140)

Take for example in the above figure, 'man', 'woman', 'king', 'queen' is represented in a vector form across multiple factors ('living being', 'human', 'royalty' etc). Here, we just have seven factors but it can be 4,000-5,000. In vector form, it will seem that man and woman are closer related whereas king and queen are closer.

The idea behind embeddings is to map words or sentences to vectors. Then, these vectors are stored in a database. New sentences can be compared to these embeddings to determine their relatedness.

With the embeddings in place, we'll initialize our vector database. Add in the codes in **bold**:

```
...

...
import ollama
from langchain_ollama import OllamaEmbeddings
from langchain_community.vectorstores import Chroma

st.title('Chat with Document') # title in our web page
loader = TextLoader('./constitution.txt') # to load text document
documents = loader.load()

text_splitter = RecursiveCharacterTextSplitter(chunk_size=1000,
chunk_overlap=200)

chunks = text_splitter.split_documents(documents)

ollama.pull('nomic-embed-text')
embeddings = OllamaEmbeddings(model='nomic-embed-text')
vector_store = Chroma.from_documents(chunks,embeddings)

# to see the chunks
st.write(chunks[0])
st.write(chunks[1])
...

...
```

Note: Before we proceed, install the relevant libraries by running:

```
pip install ollama langchain-ollama chromadb
```

We can also remove the below:
```
st.write(chunks[0])
st.write(chunks[1])

print(documents)
```

In the above, we initialize the vector store from Chroma. Chroma is an open source lightweight embeddings database that stores embeddings locally. We pass in the document chunks and the

Ollama embeddings using the *nomic-embed-text* model (you can of course use your preferred embedding model).

Next, we can setup the retrieval and querying components of our RAG app. Add some additional imports:

```
...
...
ollama.pull('nomic-embed-text')
embeddings = OllamaEmbeddings(model='nomic-embed-text')
vector_store = Chroma.from_documents(chunks,embeddings)

from langchain.prompts import ChatPromptTemplate, PromptTemplate
from langchain_core.output_parsers import StrOutputParser
```

PromptTemplate help us create structured prompts and *StrOutputParser* parses responses. We shall see their usage in the chain later.

Next import:
```
from langchain_ollama import ChatOllama
from langchain_core.runnables import RunnablePassthrough
from langchain.retrievers.multi_query import MultiQueryRetriever
```

Note: for the above imports, you need to run: *pip install langchain langchain-core langchain-community*

`MultiQueryRetriever` helps optimises our queries and streamline the retrieval process by taking our initial query and use the LLM to generate multiple relevant variant queries. These help find the best documents across all queries by looking up the relevant vectors from the vector database, and get more comprehensive search results (helps overcome limitations of simple similarity search). Add in the following:

```
llm = ChatOllama(model="llama3.2")

# a simple technique to generate multiple questions from a single
question and then retrieve documents
# based on those questions, getting the best of both worlds.

QUERY_PROMPT = PromptTemplate(
    input_variables=["question"],
    template="""You are an AI language model assistant. Your task is to
    generate five different versions of the given user question to
    retrieve relevant documents from a vector database. By generating
    multiple perspectives on the user question, your goal is to help the
    user overcome some of the limitations of the distance-based
```

```
similarity search. Provide these alternative questions separated by
newlines.
Original question: {question}""",
)

retriever = MultiQueryRetriever.from_llm(
    vector_store.as_retriever(), llm, prompt=QUERY_PROMPT
)
```

Now we're ready to create the RAG prompt that will tie everything together. Add:

```
 # RAG prompt
template = """Answer the question based ONLY on the following context:
{context}
Question: {question}
"""
```

The prompt template serves two purposes:
1. Provides clear instructions to use only the given context
2. Includes placeholders for both context and question

This will be converted into a chat prompt that combines our retrieved information with the user's question:

```
prompt = ChatPromptTemplate.from_template(template)
```

ChatPromptTemplate internally handle how to pass in the context and pull in the question, since these are received as variables. Once we've done that, we put everything into a chain.

```
chain = (
    {"context": retriever, "question": RunnablePassthrough()}
    | prompt
    | llm
    | StrOutputParser()
)
```

This process pulls together all the pieces to generate our result. We pass in the context, which comes from the retriever. The retriever knows how to get information from the vector store and works with the large language model that drives everything. It also uses the prompt we created, which includes the *content* and *question* input variables.

After assembling these components, we have the question flow through a Runnable pass-through step. Then we have a chain that processes the prompt, followed by another interaction with the large language model. Finally, we pass the result through a string output parser to clean and format everything nicely.

With all that set up, we let the user start asking questions via the StreamLit UI Frontend. Add in the codes in **bold**:

```
...
...
prompt = ChatPromptTemplate.from_template(template)

chain = (
    {"context": retriever, "question": RunnablePassthrough()}
    | prompt
    | llm
    | StrOutputParser()
)

question = st.text_input('Input your question')

if question:
    res = chain.invoke(input=(question))
    st.write(res)
```

Running our App

Let's run our app (it might take some time for the chunking and embedding) and pose a question to the US Constitution. For e.g., "What is the age requirement to be a senator?":

Chat with Document

Input your question

what is the age requirement to be a senator?

The age requirement to be a Senator is 30 years old, as stated in Article I, Section 3, Clause 3.

The answer tells us that "The age requirement to be a Senator is 30 years old, as stated in Article I, Section 3, Clause 3."

We can ask another question:

Chat with Document

Input your question

who can veto decisions made by the senate

The President of the United States can veto decisions made by the Senate. According to Section 7, every Bill that has passed both the House of Representatives and the Senate must be presented to the President before it becomes a Law. If the President approves, he shall sign it; but if not, he shall return it with his objections to the House where it originated, who will then enter those objections at large on their Journal and reconsider the bill.

Behind the scenes, the question is used to retrieve relevant documents from the vector database. It identifies pertinent documents with high similarity to keywords in the question. Once these documents are fetched, they're used, along with the model, to generate a response.

We can see the system is working successfully. We've built a RAG system using our chosen large language model, Llama 3.2, along with Ollama embeddings. Note that we have the flexibility to also swap in other LLMs and embedding models and the sytem will continue to function. This modularity is one of Ollama's strength.

Remember that our key advantage here being is cost efficiency - we can run this system as many times as needed without any API charges since everything runs locally. Currently, there's some inefficiency in our program because some unnecessary re-chunking and re-embedding of the same file exist.

We will resolve this in subsequent chapters, and also extend this application to handle PDFs and Word documents, showcasing its potential in fields like law and finance. For example, we load legal documents or financial statements, create chunks from them, embed them into a vector store, and query the documents and get the response using large language models.

Chapter 10 - Uploading Custom Documents

In this chapter, we let users upload their own documents. Add in the following codes in **bold**:

```
...
...
from langchain_ollama import OllamaEmbeddings
from langchain_community.vectorstores import Chroma

st.title('Chat with Document') # title in our web page
uploaded_file = st.file_uploader('Upload file:', type=['txt'])
...
...
```

We include a file uploader with the message "Upload file." We specify that we accept the 'txt' file type. In the next chapter, we will illustrate how to also accept multiple file types like PDF and DOCX. Once the file is uploaded, it will be stored in the *uploaded_file* variable.

Uploading and Reading the File

To read the file, add the codes in **bold**:

```
import os
...
...
st.title('Chat with Document') # title in our web page
uploaded_file = st.file_uploader('Upload file:', type=['txt'])
add_file = st.button('Add File')

if uploaded_file and add_file:
    bytes_data = uploaded_file.read()
    file_name = os.path.join('./', uploaded_file.name)
    with open(file_name,'wb') as f:
        f.write(bytes_data)

    loader = TextLoader(file_name) # to load text document
    documents = loader.load()
...
...
```

Code Explanation

```
add_file = st.button('Add File')

if uploaded_file and add_file:
```

This check ensures that the program only progresses with the file upload once the file has been specified and the add file button clicked. Without this check, the program might mistakenly attempt to upload a non-existent file resulting in errors or, it might do unnecessary repetitive chunking and embedding of the same files.

```
    bytes_data = uploaded_file.read()
```

Once the file is uploaded, its content will be read in binary format and stored in the *bytes_data* variable.

```
    file_name = os.path.join('./', uploaded_file.name)
```

The binary data will then be copied into a file in the current directory, retaining the same name as the uploaded file. You can choose to save this to any directory by specifying the desired path. This action will return the file name.

```
    with open (file_name, 'wb') as f:
        f.write(bytes_data)
```

Next, the program will open the file in binary read mode.

```
loader = TextLoader(file_name)
```

Finally in *TextLoader*, replace the hardcoding of *constitution*.txt with *file_name*.

Processing the File

At this point, the file name is supplied to our text loader. Ensure proper indentation to maintain the correct scope:

```
if uploaded_file and add_file:
    bytes_data = uploaded_file.read()
```

```python
file_name = os.path.join('./', uploaded_file.name)
with open(file_name,'wb') as f:
    f.write(bytes_data)

# move code under 'if' scope
loader = TextLoader(file_name) # to load text document
documents = loader.load()

text_splitter = RecursiveCharacterTextSplitter(...)
...

...

...

chain = (
    {"context": retriever, "question": RunnablePassthrough()}
    | prompt
    | llm
    | StrOutputParser()
)
st.success('File uploaded, chunked and embedded successfully')

question = st.text_input('Input your question')

if question:
    res = chain.invoke(input=(question))
    ...
```

If you run your code now, you will get an error like "name 'chain' is not defined":

NameError: name 'chain' is not defined

Traceback:

```
File "/Users/user/anaconda3/lib/python3.10/site-packages/streamlit/runtime/scr
    exec(code, module.__dict__)
File "/Users/user/Desktop/ollama/chatdoc2.py", line 71, in <module>
    res = chain.invoke(input=(question))
```

This is because *chain*, is now in a different scope with the below:

```python
chain = (
    ...
```

```
    )

question = st.text_input('Input your question')

if question:
    res = chain.invoke(input=(question))
    st.write(res)
```

We thus store *chain* in the session state for it to be accessible to all. Add the following in **bold**:

```
    ...

    ...
    chain = (
        ...
    )

    st.session_state.chain = chain
    st.success('File uploaded, chunked and embedded successfully')

question = st.text_input('Input your question')

if question:
    if 'chain' in st.session_state:
        chain = st.session_state.chain
        res = chain.invoke(input=(question))
        st.write(res)
```

Thus, the entire process—chunking, embedding, etc.—will only proceed if a file has been uploaded and the 'Add file' button clicked. This avoids unnecessary re-chunking and re-embedding the same file.

Now, let's save our progress and rerun the program. Browse and upload the *constitution*.txt (or your own file). We can then ask a question, such as the age requirement to become a senator.

If everything runs smoothly, it should display the correct responses.

Chat with Document

Upload file:

Drag and drop file here
Limit 200MB per file • TXT

constitution.txt 298.1KB

Add File

Input your question

what is the minimum age to be a senator

The minimum age to be a Senator is 30 years old.

In summary, we've successfully added a file upload feature for custom documents. In the following chapter, we'll extend the file uploading feature to accommodate more file types, including PDF and Word files.

In case you get lost at any point, here's the entire code:

```
import os
import streamlit as st # used to create our UI frontend
from langchain_community.document_loaders import TextLoader
from langchain.text_splitter import RecursiveCharacterTextSplitter

import ollama
from langchain_ollama import OllamaEmbeddings
from langchain_community.vectorstores import Chroma

st.title('Chat with Document') # title in our web page
uploaded_file = st.file_uploader('Upload file:', type=['txt'])
add_file = st.button('Add File')

if uploaded_file and add_file:
    bytes_data = uploaded_file.read()
    file_name = os.path.join('./', uploaded_file.name)
    with open(file_name,'wb') as f:
        f.write(bytes_data)
```

```python
loader = TextLoader(file_name) # to load text document
documents = loader.load()

text_splitter     =     RecursiveCharacterTextSplitter(chunk_size=1000,
chunk_overlap=200)

chunks = text_splitter.split_documents(documents)

ollama.pull('nomic-embed-text')
embeddings = OllamaEmbeddings(model='nomic-embed-text')
vector_store = Chroma.from_documents(chunks,embeddings)

from langchain.prompts import ChatPromptTemplate, PromptTemplate
from langchain_core.output_parsers import StrOutputParser
from langchain_ollama import ChatOllama
from langchain_core.runnables import RunnablePassthrough
from langchain.retrievers.multi_query import MultiQueryRetriever

llm = ChatOllama(model="llama3.2")

# a simple technique to generate multiple questions from a single
question and then retrieve documents
# based on those questions, getting the best of both worlds.

QUERY_PROMPT = PromptTemplate(
    input_variables=["question"],
    template="""You are an AI language model assistant. Your task is to
    generate five different versions of the given user question to retrieve
relevant  documents  from  a  vector  database.  By  generating  multiple
perspectives on the user question, your goal is to help the user overcome
some of the limitations of the distance-based similarity search. Provide
these alternative questions separated by newlines.
    Original question: {question}""",
)

retriever = MultiQueryRetriever.from_llm(
    vector_store.as_retriever(), llm, prompt=QUERY_PROMPT
)

# RAG prompt
```

88

```
template = """Answer the question based ONLY on the following context:
{context}
Question: {question}
"""

prompt = ChatPromptTemplate.from_template(template)

chain = (
    {"context": retriever, "question": RunnablePassthrough()}
    | prompt
    | llm
    | StrOutputParser()
)
st.session_state.chain = chain
st.success('File uploaded, chunked and embedded successfully')

question = st.text_input('Input your question')

if question:
    if 'chain' in st.session_state:
        chain = st.session_state.chain
        res = chain.invoke(input=(question))
        st.write(res)
```

Chapter 11 - Loading Different File Types

We'll now explore how to load different file formats, such as text files, PDFs, and Word documents, into our RAG app.

Before the code changes, we will need *pypdf* and *docx2txt* libraries to parse and extract text from these document types. Run the below to install them:

```
pip install pypdf docx2txt
```

Currently, we only accept text files, which we load via the text loader. What we'll do is examine the file extension—be it .txt, .pdf, or .doc—and use the appropriate loader based on that. Add the codes in **bold**:

```
...
...
st.title('Chat with Document') # title in our web page
uploaded_file = st.file_uploader('Upload file:',
type=['txt','pdf','docx'])
add_file = st.button('Add File')

if uploaded_file and add_file:
    bytes_data = uploaded_file.read()
    file_name = os.path.join('./', uploaded_file.name)
    with open(file_name,'wb') as f:
        f.write(bytes_data)

    name, extension = os.path.splitext(file_name)

    if extension == '.pdf':
        from langchain_community.document_loaders import PyPDFLoader
        loader = PyPDFLoader(file_name)
    elif extension == '.docx':
        from langchain_community.document_loaders import Docx2txtLoader
        loader = Docx2txtLoader(file_name)
    elif extension == '.txt':
        from langchain_community.document_loaders import TextLoader
        loader = TextLoader(file_name)
    else:
        st.write('Document format is not supported!')
```

```
documents = loader load()
```

...

...

Code Explanation

```
uploaded_file = st.file_uploader('Upload file:',
type=['txt','pdf','docx'])
```

We expand the types of documents we allow to be uploaded to *pdf* and *docx* files.

```
name, extension = os.path.splitext(file_name)
```

To extract the file extension, we utilize the *os.path.splitext()* method, where we input the filename and receive both the filename and its extension in return.

```
if extension == '.pdf':
    from langchain.document_loaders import PyPDFLoader
    loader = PyPDFLoader(file_name)
```

Based on the extension, we'll choose the corresponding loader. If the extension is *.pdf*, we'll import the PyPDFLoader, which aids in loading PDFs. Following that, we'll use *loader = PyPDFLoader* and provide the filename.

```
elif extension == '.docx':
    from langchain.document_loaders import Docx2txtLoader
    loader = Docx2txtLoader(file_name)
```

If the extension is a *.docx*, we'll utilize the `Docx2txtLoader`.

```
...
from langchain_community.document_loaders import TextLoader
...
...
    elif extension == '.txt':
        from langchain.document_loaders import TextLoader
        loader = TextLoader(file_name)
```

...

...

For a *.txt* extension, we'll use our existing *TextLoader*. We remove the duplicate import *TextLoader* statements so that we don't inadvertently import the *TextLoader* when it's not in use.

```
else:
        st.write('Document format is not supported!')

        loader = TextLoader(file_name) # to load text document
documents = loader.load()
```

There might be scenarios where a user uploads a file with an extension we don't currently support. In such cases, a notification or alert could be beneficial.

After loading, the rest of the process remains unchanged, regardless of the file type. It's just the source that varies based on the file extension.

If you're curious about adding support for a new file type or extension and need the appropriate loader, you can consult the LangChain documentation (python.langchain.com/v0.1/docs/modules/data_connection/document_loaders/). Here, you'll find a range of integrations they offer.

Displaying a Spinner While Waiting

Currently, when a user uploads a file, there's a perceivable wait time during the chunking and embedding phases. By adding a spinner with a message like "Reading, Chunking, and Embedding File", users will have a visual cue that processing is in progress. Add in **bold**:

```
...

...
if uploaded_file and add_file:
    with st.spinner('Reading, chunking and embedding file...'):
        bytes_data = uploaded_file.read()
        file_name = os.path.join('./', uploaded_file.name)
        with open(file_name,'wb') as f:
            f.write(bytes_data)
        ...

        ...
```

```
    ...
        st.session_state.chain = chain
        st.success('File uploaded, chunked and embedded successfully')

question = st.text_input('Input your question')
    ...
```

Ensure you indent the rest of the code under the spinner's scope.

Running Our App

Let's test our updates. After browsing and selecting a PDF (for instance, a user guide for SpaceX's Falcon 9 rocket) and clicking "Add File", you should observe the spinner in action:

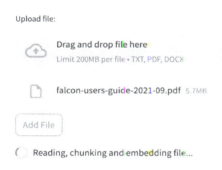

Once the file is successfully uploaded, you can proceed with inquiries like "What fuel does the Falcon 9 rocket run on?" and receive accurate answers:

Chat with Document

Upload file:

☁	**Drag and drop file here** Limit 200MB per file • TXT, PDF, DOCX	Browse files
🗋	falcon-users-guide-2021-09.pdf 5.7MB	✕

Add File

Input your question

What fuel does the Falcon 9 rocket run on?|

According to the text, the Falcon 9 rocket runs on Rocket-grade kerosene as its primary propellant.

Feel free to try this with a *.docx* file; it should work seamlessly. With these enhancements, our RAG chat-with-document app is more robust and versatile.

I hope you've gleaned valuable insights from this chapter. The potential applications span various fields, including legal, medical, scientific, and technical domains. The possibilities are boundless.

Final Words

We have gone through quite a lot of content to equip you with the skills to create Ollama LLM AI apps.

Hopefully, you have enjoyed this book and would like to learn more from me. I would love to get your feedback, learning what you liked and didn't for us to improve.

Please feel free to email me at support@i-ducate.com to get updated versions of this book.

If you didn't like the book, or if you feel that I should have covered certain additional topics, please email us to let us know. This book can only get better thanks to readers like you.

If you like the book, I would appreciate if you could leave us a review too. Thank you and all the best for your learning journey!

About the Author

Greg Lim is a technologist and author of several programming books. Greg has many years in teaching programming in tertiary institutions and he places special emphasis on learning by doing.

Contact Greg at support@i-ducate.com

www.ingramcontent.com/pod-product-compliance
Lightning Source LLC
LaVergne TN
LVHW080118070326
832902LV00015B/2656